EDEXCEL HISTORY

GCSE 9–1

Weimar and Nazi Germany 1918–39

by Paul Martin

SCHOLASTIC

Author Paul Martin

Series Editor Paul Martin

Reviewer Rosemary Rees

Editorial team Aidan Gill, Turnstone Solutions Limited, Rachel Morgan, Audrey Stokes, Kirsty Taylor, Liz Evans

Typesetting Daniel Prescott, Couper Street Type Co

Cover design Dipa Mistry

App development Hannah Barnett, Phil Crothers and RAIOSOFT International Pvt Ltd

Photographs cover and title page: © Dokumentationsarchiv des Österreichischen Widerstandes; page 10: Friedrich Ebert, Gustav Stresemann, Heinrich Brüning, Franz von Papen and Kurt von Schleicher, German Federal Archives/Wikimedia Commons; flag, Steve Allen/Shutterstock; pages 10 and 32: Paul von Hindenburg, Everett Historical/Shutterstock; page 11: Adolf Hitler, Ernst Röhm and Josef Goebbels, German Federal Archives/Wikimedia Commons; flag, Steve Allen/Shutterstock; pages 11 and 36: Herman Goering, Nicola Perscheid/Wikimedia Commons; Reinhard Heydrich, German Federal Archives/Wikimedia Commons; pages 11 and 37: Heinrich Himmler, German Federal Archives/Wikimedia Commons; page 17: bank notes as building blocks, Pictorial Press Ltd/Alamy; page 18: Gustav Stresemann, German Federal Archives/Wikimedia Commons; page 21: dancing couple, Everett Collection/Shutterstock; page 22: Bauhaus School, Lannguyen138/Wikimedia Commons; Otto Dix painting, Peter Horree/Alamy Stock Photo; Metropolis film poster, Boris Konstantinowitsch Bilinski/Wikimedia Commons; pages 24 and 70: German Day in Nuremberg 1923, INTERFOTO/Alamy Stock Photo; page 26: *Mein Kampf*, 360b/Shutterstock; page 28: Hitler, IgorGolovniov/Shutterstock; page; pages 30 and 73: Sturmabteilung (SA), INTERFOTO/Alamy Stock Photo; 32: Heinrich Brüning and Franz von Papen, German Federal Archives/Wikimedia Commons; page 33: Kurt von Schleicher, German Federal Archives/Wikimedia Commons; page 34: Reichstag Fire, Vitold Muratov/Wikimedia Commons; page 39: Nazi poster, Everett Historical/Shutterstock; page 41: Pastor Martin Niemöller, Dutch National Archives/Wikimedia Commons; pages 43, 51 and 58: Nazi propaganda poster, Peter Horree/Alamy Stock Photo; page 78 : girl sitting exam, Monkey Business Images/Shutterstock'

Illustration QBS Learning

Designed using Adobe InDesign

Published in the UK by Scholastic Education, 2020
Book End, Range Road, Witney, Oxfordshire, OX29 0YD
A division of Scholastic Limited
London – New York – Toronto – Sydney – Auckland
Mexico City – New Delhi – Hong Kong
SCHOLASTIC and associated logos are trademarks and/or registered trademarks of Scholastic Inc.
www.scholastic.co.uk
© 2020 Scholastic Limited
1 2 3 4 5 6 7 8 9   0 1 2 3 4 5 6 7 8 9

British Library Cataloguing-in-Publication Data
A catalogue record for this book is available from the British Library.

ISBN 978-1407-18339-8

Printed and bound by Bell and Bain Ltd, Glasgow
Papers used by Scholastic Limited are made from wood grown in sustainable forests.

Acknowledgements
The publishers gratefully acknowledge permission to reproduce the following copyright material: **Rob Bircher** for 'MOSFLOP' from *Germany, 1890–1945: Democracy and dictatorship* by Rob Bircher, (Scholastic Education, 2020); **Liverpool University Press** for extracts from Nazism 1919–1945 by J. Noakes and G. Pridham, (Liverpool University Press, 1984) reproduced with permission of the licensor through PLSclear; **Oxford Publishing Ltd** for extract from Backing Hitler by R. Gellately, (Oxford University Press, 2001) reproduced with permission of the licensor through PLSclear; **Randall L. Bytwerk** for extract from Nazi party election flyer; **M. Mouton** for extract from Nurturing the Nation to Purifying the Volk by M. Mouton, (Cambridge University Press, 2009) reproduced with permission of the licensor through PLSclear.

Every effort has been made to trace copyright holders for the works reproduced in this book, and the publishers apologise for any inadvertent omissions.

Note from the publisher:
Please use this product in conjunction with the official specification and sample assessment materials. Ask your teacher if you are unsure where to find them.

Contents

Features of this guide 4

Topic focus: Modern depth study 6

Timeline 8

Key figures 10

Part One: The Weimar Republic 1918–29

The origins of the Republic, 1918–19 12

The early challenges to the Republic, 1919–23 14

The recovery of the Republic, 1924–29 18

Changes in society, 1924–29 20

Part Two: Hitler's rise to power 1919–33

Early development of the Nazi Party, 1920–22 23

The lean years, 1923–29 25

The growth in support for the Nazis, 1929–32 28

How Hitler became Chancellor, 1932–33 31

Part Three: Nazi control and dictatorship 1933–39

The creation of a dictatorship, 1933–34 34

The police state 36

Controlling and influencing attitudes 39

Opposition, resistance and conformity 41

Part Four: Life in Nazi Germany 1933–39

Nazi policies towards women 43

Nazi policies towards the young 44

Employment and living standards 46

The persecution of minorities 48

How to answer the exam questions

Section A: Question 1 51

Section A: Question 2 53

Section B: Question 3 (a) 57

Section B: Question 3 (b) 61

Section B: Question 3 (c) 63

Section B: Question 3 (d) 65

Practice papers

Practice paper 1 70

Practice paper 2 73

Sources/Interpretations for practice paper 1 76

Sources/Interpretations for practice paper 2 77

Doing well in your exam   78

Glossary   80

Check your answers on the free revision app or at www.scholastic.co.uk/gcse

Features of this guide

The best way to retain information is to take an active approach to revision.

Throughout this book, you will find lots of features that will make your revision an active, successful process.

SNAPIT!

Use the Snap it! feature in the revision app to take pictures of key concepts and information. Great for revision on the go!

Regular exercise helps stimulate the brain and will help you relax.

DOIT!

Activities to embed your knowledge and understanding and prepare you for the exams.

Find methods of relaxation that work for you throughout the revision period.

NAILIT!

Succinct and vital tips on how to do well in your exam.

Words shown in **purple bold** can be found in the glossary on page 80.

STRETCHIT!

Provides content that stretches you further.

CHECKIT!

Check your knowledge at the end of a subtopic.

Revise in pairs or small groups and deliver presentations on topics to each other.

PRACTICE PAPERS

Full mock-exam papers to practise before you sit the real thing!

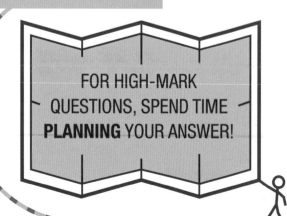

FOR HIGH-MARK QUESTIONS, SPEND TIME **PLANNING** YOUR ANSWER!

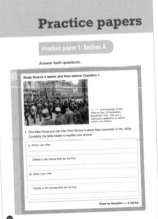
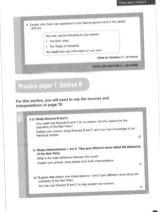

FREE REVISION APP

- The **free revision app** can be downloaded to your mobile phone (iOS and Android), making **on the go revision** easy.

- Use the revision calendar to help map out your revision in the lead-up to the exam.

- Complete multiple-choice questions and create your own **SNAP IT!** revision cards.

www.scholastic.co.uk/gcse

Online answers and additional resources
All of the tasks in this book are designed to get you thinking and to consolidate your understanding through thought and application. Therefore, it is important to write your own answers before checking. Some questions include answer lines where you need to fill in your answer in the book. Other questions require you to use a separate piece of paper so that you can draft your response and work out the best way of answering.

Get plenty of sleep, especially the night before an exam.

LOOK AFTER YOURSELF

Help your brain by looking after your whole body!

Once you have worked through a section, you can check your answers to Do it!, Stretch it!, Check it! and the exam practice papers on the app or at **www.scholastic.co.uk/gcse**.

Topic focus:
Modern depth study

This is a *Modern depth study*. You will have studied the ways in which **social**, **economic**, **political**, **cultural** and **military factors** worked together within a short time span. In Paper 3, you will face six questions on this study. The paper is worth 30% of your total GCSE and tests three different skills:

Question 1 and Question 3 (a): Source skills

You will need to analyse and evaluate contemporary **sources**. Sources provide evidence from the time you are studying, such as diaries, cartoons, newspapers, speeches or photographs.

You will need to draw **inferences** from sources: something that is implied, but not stated. You will also need to evaluate 'How useful' sources are for a given enquiry.

Observation: The Jew is shown with a communist symbol printed on a map of Germany under his arm.

Enquiry: How useful is this source for an enquiry into the treatment of minorities in Nazi Germany?

Usefulness: As a 1938 **propaganda** poster it is a clear statement of Nazi views. The fact that it is advertising an exhibition highlights another way they spread these attitudes.

Inference: The Nazis believed that Jews wanted Germany to become communist.

Usefulness: The link to communism shows how the Nazis used fear of communism to support their aims and views. It shows how Jews were made into scapegoats.

Source A: An advert for an anti-Semitic exhibition in Vienna, August 1938. The image shows a caricature (exaggerated portrayal) of a Jew and the caption reads 'The eternal Jew'.

Question 2: Causation

Your exam will have a question focused on **causation**. Question 2 asks you to 'Explain why' an event happened and will give you two prompts that you may use in your answer.

Remember causes can be *short-*, *medium-* or *long-term* and a mix of these will apply for any given event. Try to give at least three causes in your answer and explain how they link. Do not get confused with **consequences**: the *results* of an event happening.

Question 3: Interpretation skills

You will also study historical **interpretations** of events written by historians.

You will need to understand why interpretations may differ. You will also need to use evidence to support and challenge these interpretations and their conclusions, and explain 'How far' you agree.

Interpretation 1

The reason Hitler came to power in 1933 was because of the political deals of von Papen and von Schleicher with President Hindenburg. Without them, he would never have gained power.

Interpretation 2

The reason Hitler came to power in 1933 was because of the Great **Depression** and subsequent unemployment. This economic crisis led to huge support for the Nazis that could not be ignored.

How they differ:

The interpretations each give a different key reason why Hitler came to power.

Why they differ:

Interpretations may differ because:

- they focus on different sources
- they have a different historical focus (e.g. economic, political; key individuals, the masses)
- they have different perspectives (e.g. local, national; short-term, long-term)
- they have drawn different conclusions.

Evaluation:

The final question in this paper will ask you 'How far do you agree' with an interpretation's view. This question is worth over a third of the marks of the paper.

You will need to draw on your own historical knowledge to give evidence both for and against the view. You will then need to reach a conclusion to answer 'How far' you agree with it.

Timeline

The content of this topic is divided into four key topics. However, these topics overlap and it is important to understand the overall chronology of the period and the context.

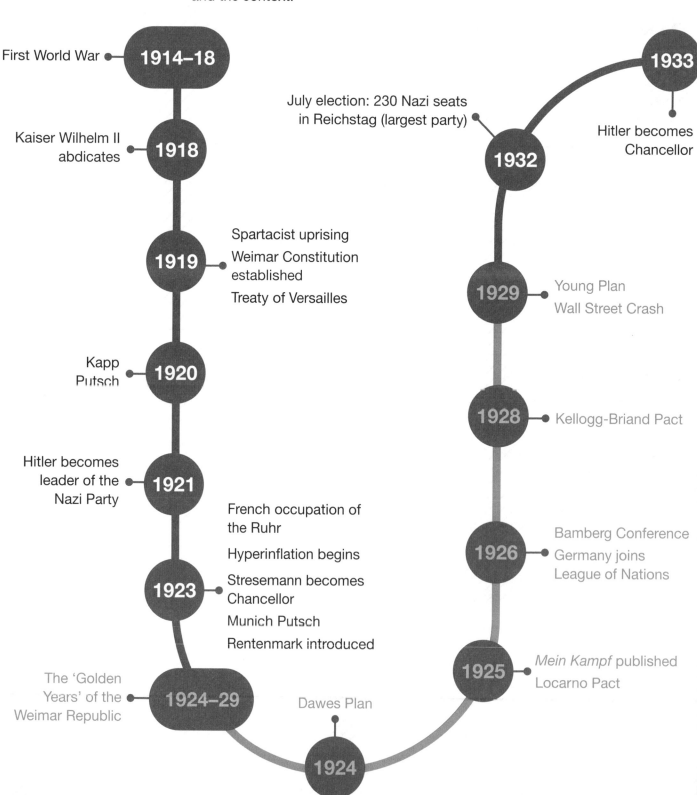

First World War • **1914–18**

1918 • Kaiser Wilhelm II abdicates

July election: 230 Nazi seats in Reichstag (largest party) • **1932**

1933

Hitler becomes Chancellor

1919 • Spartacist uprising
Weimar Constitution established
Treaty of Versailles

1929 • Young Plan
Wall Street Crash

Kapp Putsch • **1920**

1928 • Kellogg-Briand Pact

Hitler becomes leader of the Nazi Party • **1921**

1926 • Bamberg Conference
Germany joins League of Nations

1923 • French occupation of the Ruhr
Hyperinflation begins
Stresemann becomes Chancellor
Munich Putsch
Rentenmark introduced

The 'Golden Years' of the Weimar Republic • **1924–29**

1925 • *Mein Kampf* published
Locarno Pact

Dawes Plan

1924

Weimar Germany   **Third Reich**

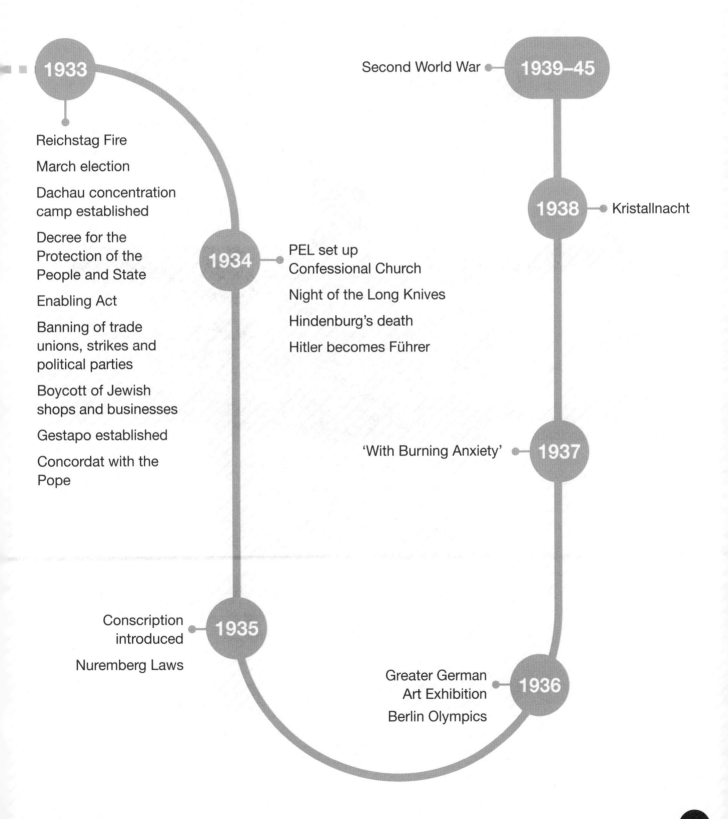

1933

Reichstag Fire

March election

Dachau concentration camp established

Decree for the Protection of the People and State

Enabling Act

Banning of trade unions, strikes and political parties

Boycott of Jewish shops and businesses

Gestapo established

Concordat with the Pope

1934

PEL set up Confessional Church

Night of the Long Knives

Hindenburg's death

Hitler becomes Führer

Second World War **1939–45**

1938 Kristallnacht

'With Burning Anxiety' **1937**

Conscription introduced **1935**

Nuremberg Laws

Greater German Art Exhibition **1936**

Berlin Olympics

Key figures

Friedrich Ebert

President of Weimar Germany, 1919–25

Leader of the Social Democrats, Ebert played a key role in drafting the Weimar Constitution.

Gustav Stresemann

German Chancellor, 1923 and Foreign Minister, 1923–29

Responsible for Germany's recovery in the 1920s, until the Great Depression.

Paul von Hindenburg

President of Germany, 1925–34

Celebrated Field Marshall who reluctantly presided over Hitler's rise to power.

Heinrich Brüning

Chancellor of Germany, 1930–32

Chancellor during the Great Depression, he was unable to govern and resigned.

Franz von Papen

Chancellor of Germany, May–Nov 1932

Kurt von Schleicher

Chancellor of Germany, Dec 1932

Both men were part of a group that tried to use and control Hitler.

Adolf Hitler

German Führer, 1934–45

*Leader of the **Nazi Party** and ruler of the German 'Third Reich', Hitler's policies led to the Second World War.*

Ernst Röhm

Leader of the SA, 1921–25, 1931–34

*The **SA** was Hitler's private army. Röhm was killed during the Night of the Long Knives.*

Heinrich Himmler

Leader of the German police, 1936–45

*Hitler's right-hand man, head of the **SS** (Hitler's guards) and chief architect of the Holocaust.*

Josef Goebbels

Minister of People's Enlightenment and Propaganda, 1933–44

Responsible for promoting Nazi ideas through media and culture.

Hermann Goering   Reinhard Heydrich

Leaders of the Gestapo, 1933–34 and 1936–42

*The Nazi secret police, the **Gestapo**, were responsible for Nazi **persecution** and terror.*

Part One:
The Weimar Republic 1918–29

The origins of the Republic

1918–1919

The legacy of the First World War

Defeat in the Great War of 1914–18 left Germany broken and divided. The **Kaiser** was forced to **abdicate** as revolution toppled the government. A new government was needed to make peace.

Impact of the First World War on Germany	• 2 million soldiers dead, over 4 million wounded • 150 billion marks in debt • Shortages of food left 750,000 German civilians dead

'The German revolution', 1918	• Strikes and demonstrations across Germany (Stuttgart, Hanover) • Workers' and soldiers' councils replaced local government • October: naval mutinies at Kiel and Hamburg • 7 November: Munich declares independence

Kaiser abdicates, 9 November 1918	• Ministers call for Kaiser to abdicate, army withdraws support • Kaiser abdicates and goes into exile on 10 November • **SPD** declares a new German Republic

Republic declared	• Chancellor Max von Baden hands over to Friedrich Ebert • Ebert agrees to work with the army to keep out **communists** • 10 November: **Reichstag** suspended, Council of People's Representatives named

Armistice signed	• 11 November: Ebert's government sign **armistice** to end fighting

Setting up the Weimar Republic

A new democratic **constitution** was agreed on 31 July 1919. To boost confidence, Ebert:

1. retained the Kaiser's civil service (government workers)
2. gained military support by promising not to reform the army
3. reassured industrialists there would be no nationalisation (state control)
4. won support from workers' **trade unions** with a promise to work for an 8-hour working day.

Born from violence and without public support, the constitution had both strengths and weaknesses as shown in the table (right):

Strengths: democratic	Weaknesses: unstable
👍 **Proportional representation:** a representative for every 60,000 votes gave all parties a chance of seats.	👎 **Proportional representation:** with 29 different parties in the 1920s, a majority was rare: coalitions were therefore needed to govern.
👍 **Extent of the franchise:** voting age dropped from 25 to 21, women included for the first time.	👎 **Article 48:** this clause allowed the Chancellor to ask the President to bypass the Reichstag when needed. It was used frequently around 1930, undermining the democratic system.
👍 **System of checks and balances:** presidential powers, Chancellor chose laws to put before Reichstag, **Reichsrat** could delay more dominant Reichstag.	👎 **Germany was still divided:** the government had relied on the army to stop riots and several parties in the Reichstag were against democracy.
👍 **Local parliaments (Länder):** controlled key services, despite stronger central government.	

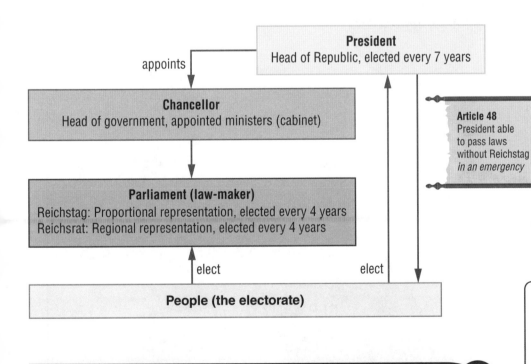

President
Head of Republic, elected every 7 years

appoints

Chancellor
Head of government, appointed ministers (cabinet)

Article 48
President able to pass laws without Reichstag *in an emergency*

Parliament (law-maker)
Reichstag: Proportional representation, elected every 4 years
Reichsrat: Regional representation, elected every 4 years

elect   elect

People (the electorate)

DOIT!

1 Annotate the diagram of the constitution (left) to show the links to its strengths and weaknesses.

2 Make a bullet list of the key problems the Weimar government faced at its creation.

STRETCHIT!

How many coalitions were there, 1919–23? What does this show about the constitution?

The early challenges to the Republic

1919–1923

Reasons for unpopularity

The end of the war and the terms of the Treaty of Versailles left much resentment in Germany. That resentment was often focused on the new government that had signed the armistice and treaty.

The *Dolchstoss*

As Germany was not invaded during the war, many Germans felt their army had not been defeated. Instead, it had been 'stabbed in the back' by the Weimar politicians. They were referred to as the 'November criminals' for signing the armistice.

The *Diktat*

The Treaty of Versailles was imposed on Germany without any discussion with German representatives. Many felt it was very harsh, so its terms were hugely resented.

Military restrictions

Soldiers: x 100,000 MAX

Navy: x 6 battleships, x 6 cruisers, x 12 destroyers, x 12 torpedo boats

Heavy artillery: NOT ALLOWED

Submarines: NOT ALLOWED

Aeroplanes: NOT ALLOWED

Rhineland demilitarised: French troops occupied until 1930

Causes of resentment

War guilt

Article 231, the 'war guilt' clause of the Treaty, made Germany accept responsibility for the war – and demanded payment of £6600 million **reparations** in compensation (set in 1921). Many Germans felt that the war was fought to *defend* Germany, that they were not to blame.

Lands lost =
50% iron ore
15% coal
15% farms
12% population
13% territory

Loss of territory

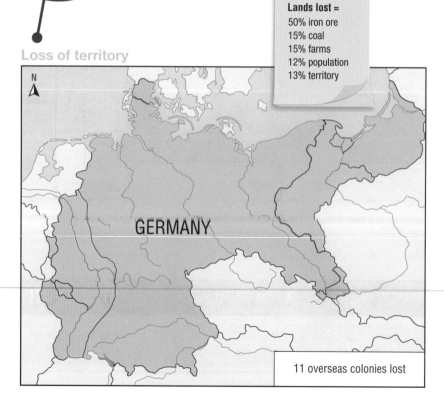

N

GERMANY

11 overseas colonies lost

Challenges from Left and Right

DOIT!

Look back over this page and score the attempts by the Left and Right to topple the government. Which side seems strongest?

1 Political challenges:

After the June 1920 elections, the moderate parties held only about 45 per cent of seats in the new Reichstag. The anti-Weimar far Right and far Left parties held about 20 per cent each.

Extreme left-wing groups:
Communist Party (KPD) *against* central government, capitalism, private ownership and enterprise.

Extreme right-wing groups:
National Party (DNVP) *for* strong government, the military, capitalism, conservatism.

2 Uprisings:

In its first two years, the Weimar government faced two serious uprisings.

Spartacist Revolt, January 1919:

The Spartacist League supported the Soviet-backed KPD. Led by Rosa Luxemburg and Karl Liebknecht, they called for a general strike and uprising in Berlin. On 6 January, they seized government newspaper and telegraph offices as 100,000 workers marched. Chancellor Ebert recruited '***Freikorps***' to crush the revolt. By 16 January, it was over and the leaders executed.

Kapp Putsch, March 1920:

When Ebert tried to disband the *Freikorps*, 5000 marched on Berlin. The army refused to fight them and the *Freikorps* took control of the city. Dr Wolfgang Kapp was declared head of a new government and the Kaiser was invited back as the Weimar government fled. Ebert encouraged trade unions to hold a national strike and Berlin ground to a halt. Unable to rule, Kapp fled and the rebellion collapsed.

3 Political violence:

Between 1919 and 1922, 376 politicians were murdered: most were left-wing or moderate.

Ten left-wing assassins were convicted and executed.

Not a single right-wing assassin was convicted, due to sympathetic judges.

The increased violence encouraged political parties to form their own armed guards to protect meetings. Even the moderate SPD formed one.

KPD set up a private army: *Rotfrontkämpfer* (Red Front Fighters).

DNVP set up a private army: *Stalhelm* (Steel Helmets).

The challenges of 1923

1923 was the low point of Weimar Germany, with a French invasion and economic crisis. The government was bankrupt: drained by war, loss of territory and reparations payments.

December 1922:	Germany failed to send reparations to France from the Ruhr coalfields.
January 1923:	French troops took control of the Ruhr industrial region and its resources.
Passive resistance:	The workers, encouraged by the government, went on strike, halting production. The government continued to pay the strikers' wages.
Impact:	The Ruhr region contained about 80% of Germany's coal, iron and steel reserves. Germany was crippled as debts and unemployment soared and goods became scarce.

Hyperinflation

The German economy could not cope with reparations payments. Income from taxation was falling as unemployment rose and factories failed. Government income was 75 per cent short of what it needed.

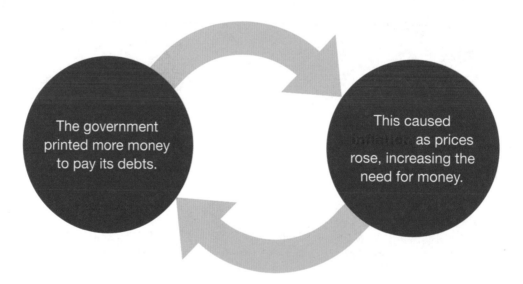

The government printed more money to pay its debts.

This caused inflation as prices rose, increasing the need for money.

The loss of the Ruhr made the situation even worse, causing **hyperinflation**.

By 1923, over 2000 printers were printing money for the government.

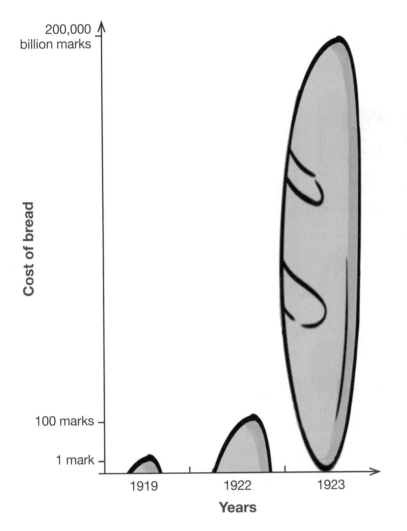

Children playing with stacks of useless German bank notes.

DOIT!

Create an advice sheet for the Weimar government on the problems it faced by 1923.

Effects of hyperinflation

There were winners and losers from hyperinflation:

Winners	Losers
✓ Farmers gained more for their produce	✗ Poorer Germans could not afford basics like food
✓ Those who had loans could repay them as their pay rose	✗ Those with savings saw their investments become worthless as prices quickly rose
✓ Those on fixed rents had more money left over	✗ Pensioners and others on fixed incomes struggled with costs
✓ Foreigners found their money went further	✗ Wage earners saw prices rise faster than their pay

NAILIT!

You need to be clear how one factor often relates to other factors. Make sure you can make links between the First World War, reparations, the occupation of the Ruhr and hyperinflation.

The recovery of the Republic

1924–1929

Economic recovery

Gustav Stresemann – Chancellor of Germany, 1923 – played a key role in the recovery of the Weimar Republic by strengthening the economy. The years 1924–29 were 'Golden Years' for the people of Germany.

The Ruhr crisis

Ended the workers' strike in September 1923, easing tensions with France and stopping the need to pay compensation to the striking workers.

Chancellor Stresemann

The Rentenmark and Reichsmark

Ended hyperinflation by introducing a new, stable currency: the **Rentenmark**.

- Set up a new, state-owned bank to issue currency in November 1923: the Rentenbank.

- Independent Reichsbank given control of currency in August 1924: renamed Reichsmark.

- Tightly controlled and backed by German gold reserves, increasing confidence and trust.

The Young Plan, 1929

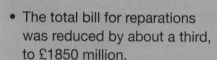

A further improvement in the reparations burden was agreed with an Allied committee led by American banker Owen Young.

- The total bill for reparations was reduced by about a third, to £1850 million.

- The timescale for repayment was increased by 59 years, to 1988.

- This allowed the government to lower taxes, boosting spending and employment.

- The French also agreed to withdraw from occupying the de-militarised Rhineland in 1930, earlier than agreed at Versailles.

The Dawes Plan, 1924

Worked with American banker Charles Dawes to resolve reparations problem.

- Payments were reduced temporarily to give the German economy breathing space.

- US banks agreed to loan money to support German industry: $25 billion, 1924–30.

- This gave the Allies confidence in repayment and so the French withdrew from the Ruhr.

Impact of economic policies

Improvements	Problems
✓ German industry's output doubled	✗ Resentment by extreme parties at agreeing again to pay reparations and until 1988!
✓ Employment and trade increased	
✓ Government income rose	✗ The economy was dependent on US loans and so remained fragile
✓ 1929 Referendum: 85% in favour of Young Plan	

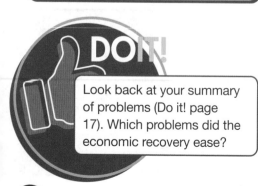

DO IT!

Look back at your summary of problems (Do it! page 17). Which problems did the economic recovery ease?

Stresemann's achievements abroad

Stresemann stepped down as Chancellor in November 1923 but remained Foreign Secretary until 1929. He dramatically improved Germany's international standing and relations.

The Locarno Pact, 1925

Signatories: Germany, Britain, France, Italy, Belgium

- Agreed with Germany, not forced upon.
- Germany accepted 1919 border with France.
- Rhineland to be permanently demilitarised.
- Talks agreed to discuss Germany joining the League of Nations (established 1920).

The Kellogg-Briand Pact, 1928

Signatories: Germany, 61 other countries, including the USA

- Agreement not to use war to resolve disputes.
- Named after French and US foreign ministers.
- The USA never joined the League of Nations and saw the Pact as a way of supporting peace in Europe.

Impact on domestic policies

These policies improved confidence in the Weimar government and boosted support for the more moderate parties in the Reichstag. This was strengthened when President Ebert died, replaced by the popular Field Marshal Paul von Hindenburg in 1925.

League of Nations, 1926

- Germany accepted as a member in September 1926.
- Germany given a place on the Council.

Positives	Negatives
✓ Germany was being treated on equal terms with other nations.	✗ The hated borders set down at Versailles had been confirmed.
✓ Tensions eased, particularly with France: Stresemann received the Nobel Peace Prize in 1926.	✗ The League was seen by extremists as a symbol of the hated Treaty of Versailles.
✓ Germany was seen as respectable and stable, a leading player once more.	✗ Germany was still bound by Versailles, including reparations and military limits.

DOIT!

1 Look back at your summary of problems (Do it! page 17). Which problems did these achievements ease?

2 Draw up a table of positives and negatives for the recovery under Stresemann. How stable was Germany by 1929, and what problems still remained?

Support for the extremist parties fell from 40 per cent in May 1924 to 28 per cent in the May 1928 elections: a drop of over a quarter.

Changes in society

Changes in the standards of living

German living standards were hard hit by the economic crises of 1918–23. From 1924, backed by the Weimar government, standards slowly improved.

1 Wages

Pay and working conditions improved:

- The average working week was reduced from 50 hours to 46 hours in 1927.
- Real wages rose by 25 per cent in the same period.

2 Housing

Following the war, there was a housing shortage of 1 million in 1923.

- In 1925, a fund for building associations was created: a 15 per cent rent tax.
- By 1929, over 100,000 new homes had been built: two-thirds by associations.

3 Unemployment

In 1924, there were 2 million unemployed people:

- By 1928, this had almost halved, dropping to 1.3 million.
- The Unemployed Insurance Act (1927) provided benefits.
- The 1920 Reich Pension Law supported over 1 million veterans, widows and bereaved.
- By 1928, the number of students in higher education had almost doubled.

Changes in the position of women

1 Work

Women's lives largely returned to how they had been pre-war. However, there was some progress:

- Booming retail and service industries provided jobs in shops and offices.
- Some professions opened up to women, such as education and medicine: the number of female doctors doubled between 1925 and 1932.

However, only 36 per cent of women in 1925 worked. Women earned on average 33 per cent less than men in similar positions and were expected to leave work when they married.

2 Politics

In November 1918, the new Weimar government gave women the vote and the right to stand in elections: by 1932, 112 women had been elected – almost 10 per cent of the Reichstag.

Article 109 of the Weimar Constitution declared equal rights and opportunities for women. However, German society was slow to change and trade unions resisted equal pay and conditions.

3 Leisure

The 1920s brought greater independence to some women, particularly young and single city workers. These 'new women' rejected traditional values in favour of having fun: drinking, smoking and dancing unaccompanied, with shorter hair, make-up and less restrictive clothing.

Some women enjoyed their new 'liberation'. Other women, and many men, felt these 'new women' undermined German society by neglecting their roles as mothers and wives:

- The annual birth rate dropped from 128 births to 80 per 1000 women, 1913–25.

- The annual divorce rate rose from 27 to 60 per 100,000 people.

Many Germans therefore felt that traditional values were under threat.

Prepare an argument for and against: 'Women's lives improved during the Weimar years.'

STRETCHIT!

Choose one of the artists named below and research their works. What do they say about Weimar Germany and German society during the 1920s?

Cultural changes

Government grants supported galleries, theatres and museums during a surge in cultural experimentation in Weimar Germany.

The easing of the restrictions of the old regime, the freedoms embedded in the new constitution and the economic recovery all helped to encourage a cultural boom.

This new energy gave rise to new ways of looking at art:

- New Objectivism rejected romantic views for realistic portrayals of modern life.
- Modernism rejected looking at the past for embracing the future and modern life.
- Expressionism encouraged artists to express their thoughts and feelings.

Architecture: The Bauhaus school, set up in 1919 by Walter Gropius, created futuristic and original designs and encouraged all types of artists to work together.

Art: Painters like Otto Dix embraced expressionism to make comments on German society, to highlight issues and make people think. Artists like Paul Klee rejected realism for abstract paintings.

Cinema: Expressionism flourished in cinema, and Germany produced new and exciting films to challenge traditional theatre: such as *Metropolis* by Fritz Lang. Actress Marlene Dietrich reflected Weimar society with her portrayals of strong female '**femme fatales**'.

CHECKIT! ✓

1 Describe three key challenges faced by the Weimar government, 1919–23.

2 Explain in a paragraph how Stresemann stabilised Germany, 1924–29.

3 Explain in a second paragraph what problems Stresemann left unresolved.

4 Describe three key changes in society in Weimar Germany, 1924–29.

Part Two:
Hitler's Rise to Power, 1919–33

Early development of the Nazis

1920–1922

DO IT!

Explain how Hitler came to dominate the DAP and Nazi Party.

Hitler's early career

Austrian Adolf Hitler moved to Munich in 1913 and fought for Germany in the First World War. Shocked by Germany's defeat and outraged by the Treaty of Versailles, he rose to prominence.

September 1919	Hitler joined the new German Workers' Party (DAP), after spying on them for the military.
January 1920	Hitler became second to Anton Drexler, in charge of propaganda.
February 1920	The Twenty-Five Point Programme written by Drexler and Hitler.
August 1920	DAP rebranded as the National Socialist German Workers' Party (NSDAP, or Nazi Party).
July 1921	Hitler challenged Drexler's leadership and took control.
August 1921	The SA were set up to strengthen Hitler's control.

Setting up the Nazi Party

1 The Twenty-Five Point Programme

This laid out the policy of the Nazi Party, and included:

- rejecting the Treaty of Versailles and building up Germany's armed forces (rearmament)
- expanding Germany's borders to provide living space (*Lebensraum*)
- excluding Jews from German society (anti-Semitism)
- nationalising industry.

NAIL IT!

There are different points of view on the reasons for the growth in support for the Nazi Party, which makes this topic a good one for interpretation questions. Remember these factors when studying the rise of the Party between 1928 and 1932.

23

2 Party organisation

Hitler introduced a number of changes to strengthen the Party:

- January 1920: Permanent office set up in Munich and a full-time administrator appointed.
- August 1920: Renaming the Party widened its appeal to both **nationalists** and **socialists**.
- The swastika logo and party salute were introduced to make the Nazis distinctive.
- December 1920: A new Party newspaper, the *People's Observer*, sold 11,000 copies.

3 Hitler's leadership and appeal

Hitler was a striking public speaker, whose energetic delivery helped attract support.

- He was the key speaker at 31 events between November 1919 and November 1920.
- In this time, membership of the Party tripled.
- He appointed loyal supporters to key positions, such as Ernst Röhm, Rudolf Hess, Hermann Goering and Julius Streicher, who became key figures in the Party.
- He made powerful friends such as the German army general, Ludendorff.

4 The role of the SA

The SA (*Sturmabteilung*) was a private army made up of unemployed former soldiers.

- Under Röhm's leadership, the SA protected Nazi rallies and disrupted opposition meetings.
- Numbering around 800 men by 1922, they gave a sense of power and organisation.
- Wearing distinctive brown uniforms, the 'Brownshirts' demonstrated military values.

By November 1923, Party membership had risen from a few thousand to around 50,000.

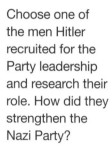

STRETCH IT!

Choose one of the men Hitler recruited for the Party leadership and research their role. How did they strengthen the Nazi Party?

DO IT!

Write a bulleted list of the key reasons for early support of the Nazi Party. How important was Hitler to their early success?

The lean years

1923–1929

The Munich Putsch

In November 1923, Hitler tried to overthrow the Weimar government in the Munich **Putsch**.

Reasons for the Munich Putsch

- Resentment over 'stab in the back' and Versailles created popular support
- Bavarian government particularly anti-Weimar and turned a blind eye to SA violence
- The Ruhr crisis and hyperinflation: Weimar government looked weak
- 1922 March on Rome by Benito Mussolini's Italian **fascists** an inspiration

8 November	• Bavarian government officials met in a beer hall in Munich.
	• Hitler and 600 SA burst in and took over at gunpoint.
	• Röhm's SA took over the local police and army headquarters.
	• General Ludendorff secretly helped the Bavarian government officials escape.

9 November	• Despite losing the support of the Bavarian government, Hitler marched on the town centre with nearly 1000 SA and 2000 additional volunteers to declare himself President of Germany.
	• The people of Munich failed to rise up and the army stayed loyal to the government.
	• Hitler was challenged by state police and firing broke out. 18 people were left dead.
	• Hitler and Goering were wounded and fled, Ludendorff and Röhm were arrested.

11 November	• Hitler was caught and arrested, having gone into hiding.

Consequences of the Putsch

Hitler had to rethink his ideas: he would have to use democracy instead.

Short-term	Long-term
Ludendorff was found not guilty.	Hitler used his trial to publicise views.
Hitler was sentenced to five years in prison.	He was released after just nine months.
The Nazi Party was banned.	The ban was lifted in 1925. Renamed, the Nazis still won 32 seats in May 1924.
Hitler was defeated and humiliated.	Hitler consolidated his ideas in *Mein Kampf*.

DO IT!

What was the key consequence of the Putsch?

The lean years, 1923–29

Hitler made use of his time in prison to firm up his ideas. After his release, he reorganised the Nazi Party in order to pursue these ideas – and to fight democratically for power.

Mein Kampf

- The Aryan (German) race was destined to rule the world.

- There was a Jewish conspiracy to stop this.

- Nationalism: Germany should be strong, reject Versailles and seize *Lebensraum* in the east.

- Socialism: wealth should benefit the workers.

- Totalitarianism: democracy was weak; strong leadership was needed.

- Traditional family values and culture to be promoted.

Reorganisation

On 27 February 1925, the Nazi Party was relaunched. Hitler reorganised it into a national party, ready to compete for seats in the Reichstag.

- The Party was organised into regions and run like a state government.

- The secretary and treasurer ensured it was well organised and funded.

- Women's and Youth movements were created to widen its appeal.

- In 1925, Röhm was replaced as head of the SA and Hitler created the SS: his elite bodyguard.

- In 1926, at the Bamberg Conference, Hitler resolved the Party split between nationalism and socialism: securing his power and the dominance of nationalist elements.

Limited support, 1924–28

By 1929, the Nazi Party was well organised and had 100,000 members. However, in the general election of May 1928, they gained only 12 seats and less than 3 per cent of the votes.

Economic stability under Stresemann, as inflation eased and unemployment declined.

Growing German international status addressed the concerns of nationalists.

Reasons for limited support for the Nazi Party

Lack of support from urban working classes, while the economy was strong.

President Hindenburg, a war hero, boosted the popularity of the Weimar government.

DO IT!

1 List five ways in which Hitler developed the Nazi Party, 1924–28.

2 Describe in a paragraph why there was only limited support for the Nazi Party, 1924–28.

The growth in support for the Nazis

1929– 1932

STRETCH IT!

Look back at the Weimar Constitution (page 13). Explain how it worsened the 1929 crisis.

The growth of unemployment

1929 marked the beginning of the end for the Weimar government: on 3 October, Stresemann died; on 24 October, the Wall Street Crash began and triggered a worldwide economic crisis – the Great Depression.

Wall Street Crash

- Falling share prices led to 'Black Tuesday' on 29 October: when 13 million shares were sold, causing panic.

- Within a week, investors had lost $4000 million: banks and businesses were ruined.

Impact on German economy

- German banks had invested heavily in US shares and suffered huge losses.

- US loans to German businesses dried up and repayment was demanded.

- The collapse of German banking caused industrial collapse as loans were called in.

- The German economy collapsed.

Rising unemployment

- In order to pay back loans, industries were forced to cut production and reduce staff.

- Global markets declined, so sales fell and further reductions were needed.

- Rising unemployment caused markets to shrink further, causing further cuts.

The initials of these seven reasons for why Nazi support increased between 1928 and 1932 spell MOSFLOP. You may find it helpful to think of an image to help you remember this.

1 Message: The Nazis focused on issues that most Germans could identify with: solving Germany's economic problems, reversing the Treaty of Versailles, making Germany great again.

2 Organisation: The Nazi Party was very well organised: orders from the top (Hitler) were carried out by enthusiastic party members throughout Germany, and the party was very good at raising money for their campaigns.

3 Strength: The Nazis' military strength (the SA) convinced many Germans that they would restore law and order in Germany and prevent a communist uprising.

DOIT!

1 Draw up a table of groups within German society in 1932. For each group, explain why the Nazi Party might have appealed to them.

2 Explain in a paragraph why support for the Nazi Party rose, 1929–32.

Impact on Germans

- The government was forced to raise taxes and cut unemployment benefits.

- Those who had invested in shares lost their savings.

- Demand for work led to lower wages: by 1932 real wages were 70% of those of 1928.

- Homelessness and crime spiralled as people became more and more desperate.

Government failure

- Chancellor Brüning proposed higher taxes and limits on benefits, but faced opposition from all sides: the Right resisted tax rises, while the Left resisted cutting benefits.

- He was unable to pass his policies through the Reichstag and relied on Presidential Decree (Article 48), issuing over 100 decrees during 1931 and 1932.

- Unable to control the Reichstag or his government, Brüning resigned in May 1932.

Rise of the KPD

- By 1932, the KPD was the largest communist party outside the USSR.

- Its support increased by around 50% 1928–32, gaining over a million voters.

- This encouraged those who feared communism to support the Nazi Party.

---

4 Fear: Votes for the KPD (communists) increased in 1928 among working-class Germans, which made many other Germans frightened of a communist takeover. The Nazis looked like the only political party that could stop this.

5 Leadership: While the Weimar government looked weak and undecided about how to tackle the Depression, Hitler was a strong leader with a clear plan.

6 Opponents: The Nazis' political opponents were the socialists (SPD) and communists (KPD). But these left-wing groups argued among themselves rather than coming up with effective anti-Nazi messages: opposition was weak.

7 Propaganda: Joseph Goebbels organised very effective propaganda for the Nazi Party. The Nazis used strong, simple messages in their posters, leaflets and radio and film broadcasts, and projected an image of strength and determination with mass rallies and marches.

Growth of Nazi support

As a result of the crisis, support for the Nazi Party increased dramatically: from 12 seats in May 1928, they won 230 seats in the Reichstag in the July 1932 elections.

The work of the SA

- Made the Nazis look strong, organised, disciplined and trustworthy.
- Could control unrest and willing to stand up to foreign powers.
- Disrupted opposition meetings: by 1930, the SA had 400,000 Storm Troopers.
- 1930 and 1932 elections were violent: the SA tore down opposition posters, intimidated candidates, raided offices and disrupted rallies. One clash in 1932 left 18 dead.

Reasons for growth in support for the Nazi Party

Appeal of Hitler and Nazis

- Strong leader who could restore order.
- Opposed the Treaty of Versailles and wanted to make Germany strong.
- Popular: he featured on posters and travelled widely, giving speeches.
- Embraced new approaches to campaigning, using aircraft and radio.
- Gained funding from wealthy businessmen opposed to communism.

Effects of propaganda: something for everyone

- Newspaper magnate Alfred Hugenberg gave them publicity in his newspapers.
- Persuaded big business leaders that they were the best hope against communism.
- Promised 'Work and Bread' to try to win the support of workers.
- Appealed to the middle classes by supporting traditional values against Weimar 'immorality'.
- Rejected the 1920 policy of nationalising private land to win over farmers.
- Targeted the young: Party rallies were exciting and colourful, the speeches stirring.
- Special appeals to women, focus on motherhood and what was best for their families.

STRETCH IT!

Research some Nazi campaign posters online. Explain which group is being targeted by each poster and how they appeal for support. What does this tell you about Nazi propaganda and support?

How Hitler became Chancellor

1932–1933

By January 1933, Hitler had become Chancellor of Germany. His rise was made possible by the political actions of three key men: President Hindenburg, Kurt von Schleicher and Franz von Papen.

Chancellor Brüning, 1930–32

March 1932 Presidential election: Hitler wins 11m votes.

April 1932 Presidential election: Hindenburg re-elected, Hitler wins 13m votes.

May 1932: Brüning bans the SA and SS to try and halt civil strife; he proposes a plan to buy land from large landowners to house the unemployed.

Chancellor von Papen, May–Nov 1932

30 May 1932: Having united the Right against him, and lost the support of landowning President Hindenburg, Brüning resigns.

Von Schleicher puts von Papen forward and suggests a coalition with Hitler, as he believes they can control the Nazis.

July 1932 elections: Nazis win 230 seats after violent clashes with communists, becoming the largest party in the Reichstag with 38% of the vote.

Hitler demands he is appointed Chancellor but Hindenburg refuses.

Chancellor von Schleicher, Dec 1932

Nov 1932 elections: Nazi seats fall to 196, but still the largest party.

Von Schleicher warns civil war will break out if von Papen stays. In December, von Schleicher becomes Chancellor, suggesting the Nazis are in decline.

Von Schleicher has no political support and cannot govern. He suggests Hindenburg makes him head of a military dictatorship instead: he refuses.

Von Papen warns of a military coup by von Schleicher. He suggests he could control Hitler if they used him as a figurehead chancellor.

Hitler becomes Chancellor

30 Jan 1933: Hindenburg reluctantly appoints Hitler as Chancellor, with von Papen as Vice Chancellor.

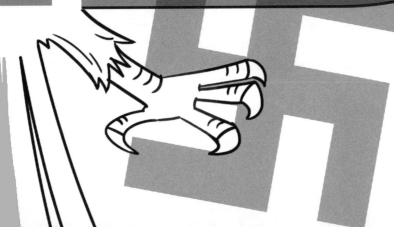

Hindenburg, Brüning, von Papen and von Schleicher

President Paul von Hindenburg

A hero of the First World War and a conservative, Hindenburg helped bring stability to the Weimar government as President, as he was popular with the Right and not one of the 'November Criminals'.

However, a monarchist and military man, he supported strong government. He made considerable use of Article 48, weakening the power of the Reichstag.

He disliked Hitler, seeing him as an upstart and common soldier. However, he allowed himself to be convinced that Hitler could be controlled and eventually appointed him Chancellor of Germany.

Chancellor Brüning

Brüning was faced with an impossible situation with the crisis of the Great Depression. However, he lost support in the Reichstag with his ban on the SA and SS, and alienated the landowning classes.

His reliance on Article 48 and failing government further undermined the Weimar Republic.

Franz von Papen

A politician and friend of Hindenburg, and right-wing conservative, keen on strong central government under the control of the landed and wealthy.

As Chancellor, von Papen gambled on holding a second election to weaken Hitler's grip on the Reichstag: although their seats did decline, the gamble failed, as the Nazi Party remained dominant.

He underestimated Hitler, describing the Nazis as children that needed hand-holding, and lifted the ban on the SA and SS in June 1932.

General Kurt von Schleicher

Chief of the German army and adviser to Hindenburg, von Schleicher was a right-wing conservative whose desire for strong, military leadership led to the rumoured coup that gave Hitler power.

Von Schleicher was behind the push to topple Brüning and abandoned von Papen when it became clear he could not govern, undermining the authority of the Reichstag.

He underestimated Hitler, believing he could control him and that the Nazis were a spent force.

DO IT!

Make a step diagram of five key events in Hitler's rise to power.

STRETCH IT!

Research von Papen and von Schleicher online. What did they have in common with each other and with President Hindenburg? What aims might they have shared with the Nazis?

CHECK IT! ✓

1 Explain in a paragraph how Hitler transformed the DAP into a credible party by 1922.

2 Explain the reasons for the Munich Putsch and its consequences for the Nazi Party.

3 Explain in a paragraph why support for the Nazis grew between 1929 and 1932.

4 Who was most to blame for Hitler becoming Chancellor, 1932–33? Explain your choice.

Part Three:
Nazi Control and Dictatorship 1933–39

NAILIT!

Hitler's rise to power is a good focus for questions on causation and on interpretations. Make sure you are clear about the order of events and the roles of individuals here.

The creation of a dictatorship

1933–1934

As soon as Hitler became Chancellor, he began working to remove any restrictions on his power. By the end of 1934, he was in complete control as the dictator of Germany: der **Führer**.

Four key events helped to cement his position and power.

1 **The Reichstag Fire, 27 February 1933**

> In the evening of 27 February, a huge fire destroyed the Reichstag building.

> Dutch communist Marinus van der Lubbe was convicted and executed.

> A communist conspiracy was blamed and 4000 communists arrested.

> Hitler persuaded Hindenburg to declare a state of emergency and new elections.

> The Decree for the Protection of the People and the State gave Hitler power to imprison opponents and ban opposition newspapers.

> The Nazis won 288 seats in a violent and bloody election campaign. The communists were banned from taking up their 81 seats, giving Hitler the majority needed to amend the constitution.

2 The Enabling Act, 23 March 1933

The Enabling Act aimed to destroy the power of the Reichstag and Hitler used SA intimidation to force the Act through: 444 votes to 94 against.

This effectively gave Hitler the right to rule without the Reichstag for four years. He used this power to remove opposition:

- Local government (Länder) was at first reorganised and then finally abolished in January 1934.

- Trade unions and strikes were banned in May 1933, with offices raided and officials arrested.

- SPD and KPD offices were raided: their newspapers destroyed and funds confiscated.

- Political parties (other than the Nazis) were finally banned in July 1933.

Law for the Removal of the Distress of the People and Reich (Enabling Act)

- Reich Cabinet can pass new laws.

- These laws can overrule the Weimar Constitution.

- Laws to be proposed by the Chancellor (Hitler).

3 The Night of the Long Knives, 30 June 1934

The last threat to Hitler came from within the Party: Ernst Röhm and the SA. Röhm and 100 other SA leaders were brutally murdered in a night of bloodshed.

The SA numbered 3 million, but were loyal to Röhm: they felt undervalued by Hitler and many were unemployed.

Röhm was on the socialist side of the party and criticised Hitler's links to the rich.

Reasons for concern

The leaders of the rival SS wanted to increase their power at the expense of the SA.

The restricted German army was dwarfed by the SA and Germany's generals felt threatened.

The leaders of the SS and the army warned Hitler that Röhm was planning a coup. On 30 June, at a meeting in Bavaria, Röhm and his senior officers were arrested, imprisoned and shot.

Vice Chancellor von Papen's staff were also arrested and his house surrounded as the SS continued to round up 'suspects'. Around 400 were murdered in total, including von Schleicher, the former Chancellor.

STRETCHIT!

Gregor Strasser was another victim of the Night of the Long Knives: research his role within the Nazi Party and why he was a threat to Hitler.

4 Hindenburg's death

On 2 August 1934, President Hindenburg – the final obstacle to Hitler holding complete power – died.

- Hitler claimed the powers of the President and declared himself Führer.

- He then forced the army to swear Oaths of Allegiance to him personally.

- On 19 August, a public vote confirmed Hitler as Führer with 90 per cent in favour.

DO IT!

1 Create a step-by-step guide to how Hitler gained total power in 1932–34.

2 List the ways in which Hitler removed or restricted opposition to his rule, 1933–34.

3 How much stronger was Hitler at the end of 1933 compared to the start of 1932?

The police state

Hitler established a police state to control the people of Germany. Three organisations spread fear of disobedience, as suspects disappeared (they were either killed or sent to **concentration camps**).

Hermann Goering

Reinhard Heydrich

1 The Gestapo

The Nazi secret police force was set up by Hermann Goering in 1933.

- In 1934, the Gestapo was placed under SS authority, under Reinhard Heydrich.

- They spied, tapped phones and used networks of informants.

- They prosecuted those who spoke out against the regime, convicting them without trial.

- Using torture to gain confessions, they sent people to prisons and concentration camps.

- In 1939, 160,000 people were arrested for political crimes.

2 The SS

Heinrich Himmler

Hitler's 'protection squad', run by Heinrich Himmler from 1929, controlled Germany's police and security forces. They were totally loyal to Hitler, and to Himmler.

- The distinctive 'Black Shirts' increased to 240,000 men in the 1930s.
- They ran the Gestapo and the SD and acted above the law.
- Himmler insisted on members only marrying 'racially pure' women.

They ran concentration camps to house political prisoners, minorities and 'undesirables'.

- By 1939, 150,000 political prisoners were in prison. Space was needed for other 'undesirables'.
- Concentration camps provided more prison space: the first camp, Dachau, opened in 1933.
- By 1939, seven large concentration camps had been built, holding around 25,000 people.
- Prisoners faced hard labour and harsh conditions, while political prisoners were 're-educated'. Many died or were broken and the camps were greatly feared.

3 The SD

A uniformed security service, set up in 1931 by Himmler and run by Reinhard Heydrich.

- Monitored opponents of the Nazi Party.
- Maintained an index of those suspected of opposition, at home or abroad.

4 The legal system

Hitler also controlled the legal system that tried and convicted his opponents:

- The National Socialist League for the Maintenance of the Law was set up: all judges had to be members and had to favour Party interests over strict application of the law.
- Trial by jury was abolished: the judge alone decided innocence, guilt and punishment.
- The People's Court was set up to hear treason cases: secret trials were presided over by hand-picked judges, with no right of appeal: 534 were condemned between 1934 and 1939.

STRETCHIT!

The Gestapo never numbered more than about 30,000 in a population of around 80 million. Their main weapon therefore was fear. Research the ways in which they spread this fear.

DOIT!

Create a spider diagram of the various ways in which Hitler's police state controlled its people.

Nazi policies towards the Churches

Nazi ideals of strength, conquest and racial purity clashed with Christian ideals of peace and cooperation. Hitler would not tolerate split loyalties and rival organisations within Germany.

1 The Catholic Church

A third of German Christians were Catholic.

Why Catholics were considered a threat to the Nazis

- Catholics were loyal to the Pope, not Hitler.
- The Catholic Centre Party was a rival political party.
- Catholic schools and youth organisations taught rival values.

Hitler agreed a Concordat with the Pope in July 1933:

- Hitler agreed to freedom of worship for Catholics and to not interfere with Catholic schools.
- The Pope agreed Catholic priests would stay out of politics.
- German bishops swore allegiance to the Nazi regime.

However, Hitler did not keep his agreement:

- Churches and monasteries were closed and Church property confiscated.
- The Church's role in education was restricted and in 1936 crucifixes were removed from schools.
- Priests were persecuted and arrested from 1935 and put on trial.
- Catholic newspapers and youth movements were suppressed.

In 1937, the Pope condemned Hitler in a statement known as 'With Burning Anxiety'. This led to increased Catholic opposition to the Nazis.

2 The Protestant Church

There were around 45 million Protestants in Germany in 1933.

- In 1933, Ludwig Müller was made 'Reich Bishop'.
- In 1936, around 2000 Protestant churches came together under Müller in the Reich Church.

Protestant pastors were encouraged to support the Nazis. Some even allowed swastikas to be displayed in their churches. People of Jewish origin were banned and the Old Testament was excluded from teaching.

DO IT!

1 Draw up a concept map of the various ways in which the Nazis attempted to control the German population. What evidence of resistance is there?

2 Did the Churches support or resist Hitler? Give two examples on each side. Once you've answered this question, see page 41 for further details about Church opposition.

Controlling and influencing attitudes

The Ministry of Propaganda

Josef Goebbels was Hitler's Chief Propaganda Minister. Through propaganda and **censorship** the Nazis sought to control and influence public attitudes in Germany.

Media: the press

- Journalists faced censorship and were given briefings with instructions on what to write.
- Newspapers that failed to follow Nazi instructions were closed down: 1600 in 1935 alone.

Media: the radio

- All radio stations were put under Nazi control and officials made regular broadcasts.
- Cheap, mass-produced radios were sold widely – with short ranges to avoid foreign stations.
- Radios were found in schools, factories and homes: 70% of homes had a radio in 1939.

Propaganda methods

Media: cinema

- All films were preceded by a 45-minute government update of its achievements.
- This brought Nazi messages to millions of cinema-goers (250 million in 1933 alone).

Posters

- Propaganda posters were widely circulated and often featured Hitler.
- The 'cult of Hitler' promoted him as a hard-working, 'superman' saviour.

Rallies

- Rallies and parades were held across the country to demonstrate Nazi strength and unity.
- Mass rallies were held annually at Nuremberg in a purpose-built staging area.
- The 1934 Nuremberg rally was featured in the propaganda film *Triumph of the Will*.

Sport

- Teams were made to salute and stadiums were covered in Nazi symbols to 'Nazify' success.
- The 1936 Berlin Olympics were a showcase for Nazi efficiency and success.
- A purpose-built stadium (the biggest in the world) was built for the event.

STRETCHIT!

1. Research the 'Cathedral of Light' used at the Nuremberg rallies.

2. Research German success at the Berlin Olympics.

How were these events used to promote Nazi ideals?

Nazi control of culture and the arts

Goebbels set up the Reich Chamber of Culture in 1933, part of his Ministry of Propaganda, in order to ensure the '**Nazification**' of German culture.

- All workers in the media and the arts had to be members of the Chamber.
- Only those sympathetic to the Nazi Party were granted membership.
- The Chamber controlled the press, radio, film, literature, theatre, music and art.
- Cultural activities that encouraged traditional values and Nazi ideals were encouraged.

Chamber of the Visual Arts

- All painters and sculptors had to become members in order to teach or produce art.
- Studios and galleries were inspected: in 1936, over 12,000 art pieces were removed.
- The Greater German Art Exhibition was held in 1936.

Architecture

- The Nazis rejected Weimar architecture in favour of classical, powerful designs – such as that used in Ancient Rome and Greece.
- Albert Speer, a favourite architect of Hitler's, designed the Nuremberg rally site and Hitler's offices.

Control of the arts

Literature

- Books could not be published without approval and existing books were censored.
- 2500 authors' works were banned and millions of books were burned in public book burnings.

Music

- 'Degenerate' music, such as jazz and the work of Jewish composers such as Mendelssohn, were banned.
- Traditional music, such as that of Wagner, Beethoven and Bach, was promoted.

Film

- Plot details for all new films had to be approved by Goebbels.
- The Nazi Party made around 1300 films, mixing entertainment with propaganda.

DOIT!

Was Nazi cultural policy about controlling or creating art? Give two arguments for each.

NAILIT!

Nazi propaganda was often expressed through posters and art. Practise extracting inferences on Nazi values and beliefs from images you come across in your revision.

Opposition, resistance and conformity

The extent of support for the Nazi regime

Hitler came to power with significant popular support: he came a close second in the last presidential election (with over a third of the vote) and the Nazis were the largest party in the Reichstag. This conformity or acceptance continued throughout the 1930s.

- Criticism of the Nazis was banned; Goebbels' propaganda ensured Hitler remained popular.

- Nazi success in reducing unemployment and challenging Versailles was also very popular.

- Fear of the Gestapo and concentration camps also encouraged conformity.

It is difficult to know how far this support was genuine or reluctant. However, there were some people who did actively oppose the Nazi regime.

Opposition from the Churches

1 A 'Confessional Church' was set up in 1934 by Martin Niemöller and the Pastors' Emergency League (PEL), to rival the Nazi Reich Church. 6000 Protestant pastors joined and 800 of them were sent to concentration camps.

STRETCHIT!

Read Niemöller's 'Confession' speech of 1946. List each of the opponents of the Nazis he names and state how they were silenced. How does this explain the limited resistance?

Martin Niemöller

A German U-boat commander in the First World War, he opposed the 1920s Weimar government.

- He voted for the Nazi Party and welcomed Hitler's appointment as Chancellor.
- He objected to Nazi interference in Church affairs and set up the PEL in 1933.
- He objected to the ban on baptising Jews, though not other restrictions on them.
- After a series of arrests, he was sent to a concentration camp in 1938.
- He offered to fight for Germany if he was released in 1939, but stayed until 1945.

Niemöller famously preached a sermon about how he did not speak out until 'they' came for him, by which time it was too late as there was no one left to speak for him.

2 The Pastors' Emergency League (PEL) opposed two key Nazi policies:

- Joining the regional Protestant churches into one national Church.

- Banning people of Jewish origin from becoming Christian and teaching the Old Testament of the Bible used in Judaism.

3 Some Catholic priests also spoke out against Hitler and the Nazis, especially after the Pope condemned Hitler (see page 38). Around 400 were sent to the 'Priest's Block' at Dachau concentration camp.

DOIT!

Was Church opposition about interference or Nazi policies? Give a piece of evidence to support each choice.

Opposition from the young

The Nazi youth programme expanded to include all young people. The state organised everything for its own benefit and freedoms were limited: some rebellious youths formed alternative groups.

① The Swing Youth

- Mainly middle-class teenagers from big towns and cities.
- Admired American culture: clothes, films, music.
- Gathered to drink, smoke and listen to music.
- Organised illegal dances, some attended by thousands of youths.

② The Edelweiss Pirates

- Gestapo files in Cologne named over 3000 teenagers as Pirates.
- Escaped restrictions on long hikes and camping trips.
- Taunted and attacked Hitler Youth members.
- Local working-class 'gangs' of teenagers from the big cities.
- Resented military discipline and lack of freedom of Hitler Youth.
- Wore their hair long and adopted American fashions.

③ Impact

Youth opposition had limited impact on Nazi Germany to 1939:

- Aside from resisting Nazi conformity, their actions were limited to social disturbances such as graffiti, jokes and attacking Hitler Youth members.
- They were mainly cultural movements, wanting freedom of expression.
- Their numbers paled against roughly 8 million members of the Hitler Youth.

CHECK IT!

1. Give a step-by-step explanation of Hitler's rise from Chancellor to Führer, 1933–34.

2. Describe three ways in which the Nazi Party controlled the German people.

3. Describe five methods by which Goebbels controlled attitudes towards the Nazis.

4. Explain two ways in which the Churches and two ways in which youth resisted Hitler.

Part Four:
Life in Nazi Germany 1933–39

Nazi policies towards women

Nazi Germany promoted the traditional view of women as mothers and housewives, and their importance in raising loyal supporters of the Nazi regime, against the Weimar 'new women'. Nazi policies aimed at increasing the birth rate and removing women from the workplace.

DOIT!

Link each of the Nazi views on women below with a policy that helped encourage it.

Appearance: 'natural' look – long, tied-back hair and no make-up.

Aryan: blonde hair and blue eyes was the 'racially pure' ideal.

Employment: men were the breadwinners, so women need not work or study.

Nazi views on women and the family

Clothing: traditional and modest, with long skirts or dresses.

Role: to stay home and raise a family, domestic skills.

The Three Ks: Kinder, Küche, Kirche (Children, Kitchen, Church).

Nazi policies towards women

In 1934, Gertrud Scholtz-Klink was appointed a Reich's Women's Leader to push Nazi views. The German Women's Enterprise incorporated all women's organisations under Nazi control, running courses on childcare, cooking and sowing for its 6 million members.

Nazi policies tried to ensure that women played the role in society the Nazis believed they should:

- The Law for the Encouragement of Marriage (1933) offered marriage loans to young couples, provided the wife gave up work. Every child the couple had reduced repayment by a quarter.

- The Mother's Cross medals were issued to women who bore four or more children. Gold-medal women were saluted by the Hitler Youth.

- Women were banned from working as teachers, doctors and civil servants (1933), and becoming a judge or lawyer, or even sitting on a jury (1936).

- Grammar schools for girls, preparing for university, were banned in 1937.

 STRETCHIT!

Research Himmler's Lebensborn programme. What does this reveal about Nazi attitudes?

Research Scholtz-Klink's life and career. In what ways did she live up to Nazi values?

Nazi policies towards the young

The Hitler Youth and League of German Maidens

Hitler was determined to create a 'thousand-year' Reich (empire): in order to groom the young into devoted Nazis for the future, the Nazis created youth groups to instil Nazi ideals.

Rival youth groups were banned from 1933, sports facilities were taken over by the Hitler Youth to encourage membership and membership from age 10 became compulsory in 1939.

1 Hitler Youth

Boys aged 6–10 could join the *Pimpfe* (Little Fellows); boys aged 10–14 joined the *Deutsche Jungvolk* (German Young People); they then joined the *Hitler Jugend* (Hitler Youth) until 18.

Character training
Activities built comradeship, loyalty, competitiveness and ruthlessness, with harsh punishments.

Political training
Boys swore loyalty to Hitler, learned about Nazi ideals and were encouraged to act as spies.

Training

Military training
Boys learned map-reading, signalling, shooting and were divided into specialist divisions.

Physical training
Regular camping, hiking and sports competitions helped build healthy soldiers for Hitler.

2 League of German Maidens

Girls aged 10–14 joined the *Jungmädel* (Young Maidens); they then joined the League until aged 21.

Political training
Girls also took part in political training, such as rallies, and swore allegiance to Hitler.

Physical training
Activities to build character and physical health prepared girls for motherhood.

Training

Racial hygiene
The importance of racial purity and only marrying Aryans was taught.

Domestic training
Girls learned household skills such as cooking, sewing, ironing and making beds.

Nazi control of education

In 1934, Bernhard Rust was appointed Education Minister. By controlling teachers and the curriculum, he intended to use education to create loyal Nazis for the future.

1 Controlling teachers

- In April 1933, the Nazis had passed a law enabling them to sack undesirable teachers. In Prussia alone, Rust removed over 180 teachers.
- The Nazi Teachers' League taught Nazi ideals in political education courses for teachers.
- All teachers had to join the League and swear loyalty to Hitler.
- From 1935, only Nazi-approved textbooks were allowed.

2 Propaganda in schools

- Lessons started and ended with 'Heil Hitler' and the Nazi salute.
- Nazi banners and posters decorated classrooms.
- German history, Nazi racial ideas and anti-Semitism were embedded into subjects.
- School radios broadcast key political messages.

3 Curriculum changes

- New subjects taught Nazi racial ideas and eugenics: the science of selective breeding.
- Time spent on physical education doubled to one-sixth of lesson time.
- Domestic science, including cookery and needlework, was compulsory for girls.
- Boxing became compulsory for boys, while maths and chemistry included topics such as poison gases, explosives, bombing and the cost to the state of the disabled.

STRETCHIT!

Research Rust's Napolas schools. How did these prepare future German leaders?

DOIT!

1 Describe in a paragraph how Nazi education prepared boys and girls to serve Nazi Germany.

2 Nazi policy aimed at turning Germany's youth into future soldiers and mothers, loyal to the Nazi regime. List five ways in which boys and girls were prepared for these roles.

NAILIT!

Think about what sources might support each topic. How useful would a school timetable be for an enquiry into Nazi education policies on attitudes towards the role of women?

Employment and living standards

Nazi policies to reduce unemployment

Hitler came into power on a wave of discontent following the Great Depression. He was determined to reduce the 6 million unemployed so they could contribute to society and would not join the KPD.

1 Labour Service (RAD)

From 1933, the National Labour Service provided paid employment for the unemployed.

- Originally voluntary, six months' work became compulsory for young men.
- Provided public services such as fixing roads and draining marshes.
- Military discipline, low pay and poor conditions made service unpopular.

2 Autobahns and public works

Public works developed German infrastructure and provided many jobs in construction.

- The **autobahn** project to build 7000 miles of roads around Germany employed 125,000 men.
- Spending on public works doubled as buildings, bridges and sports facilities were created.
- Better transport links boosted German industry and agriculture.

3 Rearmament

Hitler was determined to break the terms of the Treaty of Versailles and rebuild Germany's forces.

- Military conscription was introduced in 1935: over a million men were in the German armed forces by 1939.
- Government arms spending jumped from 3.5 billion to 26 billion marks, 1933–39.
- People employed in the aircraft industry jumped from 4000 in 1933 to 72,000 by 1935.

4 'Invisible employment'

Unemployment had dropped by 1939 to only 0.3 million. However, the Nazis left out certain groups in their calculations.

- Women and Jews forced out of work were not counted.
- Labour Service workers and those working on public works were excluded.
- The hundreds of thousands sent to prisons or concentration camps were not counted.
- Part-time workers were counted as fully employed.

DO IT!

LAIR: Labour Service, Autobahns, Invisibles, Rearmament. Think up other mnemonics or images to help you remember information and take snapshots to test your memory.

Changes in standards of living

The Nazi economy was run foremost to benefit the state. However, Hitler knew it also had to improve the lives of workers if he was to stay in power.

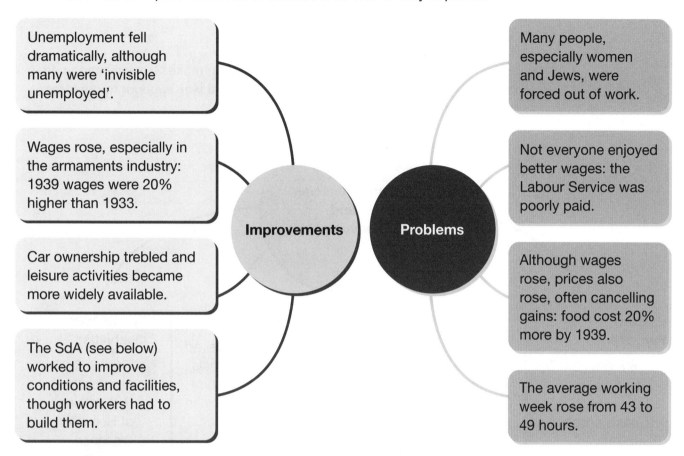

Improvements

Unemployment fell dramatically, although many were 'invisible unemployed'.

Wages rose, especially in the armaments industry: 1939 wages were 20% higher than 1933.

Car ownership trebled and leisure activities became more widely available.

The SdA (see below) worked to improve conditions and facilities, though workers had to build them.

Problems

Many people, especially women and Jews, were forced out of work.

Not everyone enjoyed better wages: the Labour Service was poorly paid.

Although wages rose, prices also rose, often cancelling gains: food cost 20% more by 1939.

The average working week rose from 43 to 49 hours.

Workers' organisations were set up to improve people's lives:

1 German Labour Front (DAF)

- Replaced trade unions and protected the rights of workers.
- Workers lost their right to negotiate improved pay and conditions.
- Punishments were issued to those who disrupted production.

2 Strength through Joy (KdF)

- Provided low-cost leisure activities to reward workers, such as sports events, films, holidays.
- Ran the 'People's Car' scheme to help workers save for an affordable car, the Volkswagen.
- The factories set up with the savings were turned to producing arms instead in 1938.

3 Beauty of Labour (SdA)

- Campaigned for better facilities for workers, such as toilets, showers and canteens.
- Employers were given tax breaks to help fund these improvements.
- However, workers were expected to volunteer their spare time to build and decorate these.

DO IT!

1 Describe three ways in which workers were better off under Hitler's regime.

2 Describe three ways in which workers were worse off under Hitler's regime.

3 'Hitler's Germany enjoyed an economic boom.' Explain in a paragraph how far you agree or disagree with this statement.

The persecution of minorities

Nazi racial beliefs and policies

Hitler wanted to 'purify' the German race to help make Germany strong again: the Nazis believed in an Aryan 'master race' that was superior to other races and was therefore set above them.

Untermenschen and Lebensunwertes

Eastern Europeans

- The Slavs from Eastern Europe were seen as 'Untermenschen', 'sub-human'.
- Hitler wished to carve out 'Lebensraum', 'living space' from their countries.
- German Slavs were constantly reminded that they were 'lesser beings' than Aryans.

'Gypsies'

- The roaming Roma and Sinti 'gypsies' were seen as work-shy and lazy, a threat to racial purity.
- They were labelled 'Lebensunwertes', 'unworthy of life'.
- From 1933, 'gypsies' were rounded up and sent to concentration camps.
- From 1938, 'gypsies' were registered and tested for purity in order to remain citizens.
- In 1939, orders were issued to begin deporting all 'gypsies' to Poland.

Homosexuals

- The Nazis believed that homosexuals were immoral and a threat to German purity.
- Laws against homosexuality were tightened: 8000 gay men were arrested in 1938.
- After serving prison sentences, gay men were often sent to concentration camps: 5000 died in camps.
- The voluntary **castration** of gay men was encouraged by Nazi laws.

People with disabilities

- The 1933 Law for the Prevention of Hereditary Diseased Offspring enforced the **sterilisation** of 400,000 mentally and physically disabled people by 1939.
- In 1939, the T4 programme began killing babies and children up to age 17 with disabilities.

DO IT!

List three ways that Nazi racial policies tied into other policies to strengthen the state.

The 1935 Nuremberg Laws banned Aryans from marrying 'undesirables' and mixed-race children were sterilised in an attempt to purify the Aryan race. Aryan 'race farms' encouraged pure breeding.

The persecution of the Jews

At the bottom of the Nazi racial hierarchy were Jews, who Hitler held responsible for all of Germany's woes. Mounting persecution led eventually to the horrors of the Holocaust.

Historical: Jewish customs and looks stood out, Jews were often successful businessmen.

Religious: They practised a different religion and Christians blamed them for Christ's death.

Nazi propaganda: Encouraged Germans to turn a blind eye to or even participate in persecution.

Causes of anti-Semitism

Nationalism: Germany was newly unified and nationalism focused attention on 'enemies'.

Scapegoats: They were blamed for 'undermining' Germany from within.

Communist conspiracy: Karl Marx, founder of communism, was Jewish – guilt by association.

Building persecution of Jews

1933	Banned from government, civil servants and teachers sacked. Banned from inheriting land. Boycott of Jewish shops and businesses enforced by the SA (30 March).
1934	Some local councils banned Jews from parks and swimming pools: 'Jewish' benches painted yellow.
1935	Banned from the army, despite several First World War war heroes being Jewish. The Nuremberg Laws (15 September).
1936	Banned from working as vets, accountants, dentists and nurses.
1937	Jewish businesses taken over. Jews identified on passports and given added names to identify them.
1938	Had to register property and carry identity cards. Kristallnacht (9 November).
1939	Banned from owning businesses. Reich Office for Jewish Emigration set up to expel Jews.

The Nuremberg Laws, 1935

On 15 September 1935, two new laws increased the persecution of Jews.

The Reich Law on Citizenship

- Only those with German blood were German citizens.
- Jews were 'subjects' not 'citizens'.
- Jews therefore could not vote, hold office or hold a passport.
- They had to wear a yellow star in order to be easily identified.

The Reich Law for the Protection of German Blood and Honour

- Jews forbidden from marrying German citizens.
- Jews forbidden from having sex with German citizens.

DOIT!

Compare the timeline of Jewish persecution to the persecution of other minorities. Describe how the persecution changed as Germany moved closer to war.

Anyone with at least three practising Jewish grandparents was considered a Jew.

Kristallnacht

On the night of 9 November 1938, hundreds of Jewish homes, shops and synagogues were destroyed in the 'Night of the Broken Glass', named for the shattered glass in the streets.

7 November: German shot in Paris embassy by a young Jew.

8 November: Goebbels stirs up retaliation in Hanover against local Jews.

Overnight: Around 100 Jews are killed, over 800 shops, 170 homes and 190 synagogues are destroyed by uniformed and non-uniformed groups. The police are told to stay away.

9 November: First victim dies. Goebbels and Hitler turn violence into a nationwide campaign.

Aftermath: The Jews are blamed by Goebbels and fined 1 billion marks to pay for the damage. 20,000 Jews are arrested.

✓ CHECKIT!

1 Describe in a paragraph how Nazi policies on women and youth aimed to encourage the development of a new generation of loyal Nazis.

2 Explain in a paragraph how Weimar 'new women' differed from the Nazi ideal and how women's status changed during the Nazi regime.

3 'Life in Nazi Germany improved for working people.' Give three arguments in support of this statement and three against.

4 Describe in a paragraph the impact of Nazi racial theory on minorities in Germany.

How to answer the exam questions

Section A: Question 1

 Give **two** things you can infer from Source A about…

You will be given a table to complete for this question. You will need to give two **inferences** from the given source and to give details from the source that back up each of your inferences.

As the question is only worth 4 marks, you need to be concise and focused in your answer: keep it brief. Do not write more than is necessary!

A strong, Aryan man stands above his family.

A smiling mother sits with her two youngest children.

A Hitler Youth in uniform stands beside his father.

The three male figures all stare forwards, with deep blue eyes and blonde hair.

A young girl's attention is on her mother and baby sibling.

A young boy, smartly dressed, stands beside his father.

Nazi propaganda poster promoting annual Winter Relief work in 1938. The caption reads 'Winter Relief Work: A people helps itself'.

DOIT!

1 Which details could you use to support each inference below?

> The Nazis believed women should focus on raising large families.

> The Nazis believed in promoting the purity and superiority of the Aryan race.

> The Nazis believed boys should become strong, loyal Nazi soldiers.

> The Nazis believed that the male role was that of leader and provider for his family.

2 What inference could you draw from the poster caption?

3 Pictures are a memorable way of recalling information. Draw a copy of a picture such as the source above and annotate it with links to key topics to jog your memory.

How many links can you add?

The sources in the exam could either be images or text. It is important to practise analysing both. Key phrases are highlighted in the source below.

Edexcel exam-style question

Study Source A below and then answer Question 1.

Source A: Extract from Hitler's speech to the National Socialist Women's League, 8 September 1934.

> If the man's world is said to be the State, his struggle, his readiness to devote his powers to…the community, then it may perhaps be said that the woman's is a smaller world. For her world is her husband, her family, her children, and her home. But what would become of the greater world if there were no one to tend and care for the smaller one? How could the greater world survive if there were no one to make the cares of the smaller world the content of their lives? No, the greater world is built on the foundation of this smaller world.

1 Give **two** things you can infer from Source A about Hitler's views on family roles. Complete the table below to explain your answer.

(i) What I can infer:

....

....

....

Details in the source that tell me this:

....

....

....

(ii) What I can infer:

....

....

....

Details in the source that tell me this:

....

....

....

(Total for Question 1 = 4 marks)

Here are some student notes to answer this question:

- Man to govern and fight: 'State', 'struggle'. Woman to raise family.
- Equal but different.

DO IT!

Write two more inferences, with evidence, to answer the question above.

The mark scheme awards one mark each for two relevant inferences and an additional mark each for relevant evidence to support the inferences.

Hitler believed boys should be raised to become loyal Nazi soldiers, ready to fight for and serve Germany. (1) He says their world is 'the State', suggesting politics, and 'his struggle', suggesting fighting. (1)

Section A: Question 2

 Explain why...

You need to demonstrate your **knowledge and understanding** of relevant historical features as well as your ability to **analyse causation** in this question. You will be provided with two prompts that you may include: but be sure to include at least one more feature in order to access the higher marks.

The question is worth 12 marks, roughly a quarter of the paper. Aim to give at least **three** reasons and make sure you explain how they led to the result in question.

Below are some key events and some of their causal factors.

Key events		
Resentment at Weimar government	Rise of the Nazi Party	Hitler becomes Führer
Recovery of the Weimar Republic	Hitler becomes Chancellor	Fall in unemployment, 1933–39

Causal factors		
Retenmark	Treaty of Versailles	Appeal of Hitler
Brüning resignation	Death of Hindenburg	Presidential election
Unemployment	Labour Service	Dawes Plan
'Stab in the back' myth	Rearmament	Reichstag Fire

1 Identify the pair of causes that relate to each of the key events above.

2 Identify a third cause for each key event.

3 Write a paragraph that links each cause into an explanation for how one event happened.

NAIL IT!

Lists are a good way of managing information for recall. Identify as many key events as you can in this topic and draw up a list of 3–5 causes for each event. This will be good preparation for your causation question. Remember not just to list the causes but to explain how they are linked.

Often events will have long-term causes, medium-term causes and shorter-term trigger causes. It is important to show how each cause feeds into the next to build to the end result.

Here are some causes and consequences of Nazi anti-Semitism:

1933 boycott	Exclusion from roles	Segregation	Cultural differences
Religious differences	Nuremberg Laws	Nazi racial attitudes	1939 eviction order
Mein Kampf	Nationalism	1 billion mark fine	Scapegoats
20,000 Jews sent to concentration camps	Nazi propaganda	Jealousy	*Kristallnacht*

DO IT!

1 Identify the causes of Nazi anti-Semitism in the list above.

2 Reorder the causes into long-term, medium-term and short-term.

3 Write a three-paragraph explanation of causes of anti-Semitism using at least five of the causes.

It is important to structure your answer and to link back to the question or topic clearly to show that you are focused on the topic in hand. Look at the notes below for one student's essay plan. Try incorporating these sentence starters into your answer:

- Introduction: Nazi anti-Semitism built on historical prejudices in Germany at the time, but there were further medium-term and shorter-term causes as well.
- The historical causes of anti-Semitism were…
- The aftermath of the First World War gave more excuses for anti-Semitism because…
- Hitler developed his reasons for Nazi anti-Semitism…
- Conclusion:

DO IT!

1 Write a short conclusion to complete the above essay plan.

2 Rewrite your three-paragraph explanation of causes of anti-Semitism using the structure above.

NAIL IT!

Remember to use the language of causation to link your paragraphs and relate your answer to the question: a reason for this was; this was caused by; this led to; a number of factors were responsible.

Look at the exam-style question below.

Edexcel exam-style question

2 Explain why there was only limited opposition to Hitler, 1933–39.

> You may use the following in your answer:
> - Enabling Act
> - The SS
>
> You **must** also use information of your own.

(Total for Question 2 = 12 marks)

The mark scheme divides the 12 marks evenly between knowledge and understanding and analysis of causation. A strong answer will show a coherent focus on the question and accurate, relevant supporting information.

Here are some student notes to answer this question:

- Enabling Act, March 1933: led to banning of Trade Unions, political parties
- The SS - Night of the Long Knives, 1936 Police State (Gestapo, SD)
- Controlling religious views
- Controlling and influencing attitudes

DO IT!

1 Add supporting detail to the last two points in the student plan above. You need to show relevant historical knowledge to back up your reasons in the exam.

2 Choose one of the last two points and write a paragraph explaining how it limited opposition to Hitler. Remember to refer back to the question wording.

3 Now try to write a complete answer to the exam-style question above.

NAIL IT!

According to the mark scheme, a strong answer should:

- give an explanation focused on *analysing* why
- be coherent, sustained and well structured
- provide accurate and relevant information
- show wide-ranging knowledge and understanding of the topic concerned.

Does yours?

Compare your answer to the question on the previous page about why there was only limited opposition to Hitler with the following student answer.

In August 1934, President Hindenburg died, leaving Hitler to assume complete control as Führer of Germany. He used his power in many ways in order to limit opposition to his total rule.

The Enabling Act of March 1933 allowed Hitler to pass laws without challenge. He used this to attack directly challenges to his power in order to limit opposition. In May 1933, the Nazis attacked Trade Unions, breaking into their offices and arresting officials. The unions were banned and strikes became illegal. Political Parties were also targeted, further limiting avenues for opposition: the offices of the SDP and KDP were attacked, their newspapers destroyed and their funds taken. In July 1933, the Law against the Establishment of Parties made Germany a one-party state.

Another reason for limited opposition was Hitler's use of the SS to remove opposition from within the Party and to set up a police state to control Germany. In 1934, leaders of the SA (including Röhm) were murdered in the Night of the Long Knives - removing at a stroke a strong potential rival and his powerbase. By 1936, the SS had become the head of a unified police and security force. Often acting beyond the law, the Gestapo spread fear through their network of informants, discouraging disloyalty, while the SD monitored all opposition. Those in opposition soon found themselves facing prison or concentration camps, limiting opposition further by spreading fear of the consequences.

The Churches were another source of opposition that Hitler acted to limit. In July 1933, he signed a 'Concordat' with the Pope, in which the Catholic Church ordered its priests to stay out of political matters. The German bishops had to swear oaths of loyalty to the Nazi regime. This limited the freedom of Catholic Church leaders to speak out against the Nazis. In 1936, Hitler set up the Reich Church under Ludwig Müller in order to limit opposition in the Protestant Churches. Only Protestant pastors who supported the regime could preach in this Church and some displayed Nazi symbols as well. In this way Protestant opposition was limited.

As Hitler had done with propaganda in order to gain popularity he targeted different areas of opposition in turn in order to limit opposition. As Pastor Niemöller commented, when they came for him there was no one left to object.

Note how the student has linked their answer back to the question throughout. Note also where they have added supporting details and given a third reason as well as using the prompts.

DO IT!

Which of the following levels from the mark scheme would you give this answer?

Level 1 Simple and general answer, lacking development, organisation and own knowledge.

Level 2 Limited analysis, with only some focus, development, organisation and knowledge.

Level 3 Analytical explanation is mostly focused and well organised, accurate and relevant knowledge shown.

Level 4 Analytical explanation is consistently focused and well organised, accurate and relevant knowledge directly addresses the question.

STRETCH IT!

Try writing your own causation questions for friends to answer. How many topics can you write one for? Don't forget to include a couple of prompts for each

Section B: Question 3 (a)

How useful are Sources B and C…

You will be asked to **evaluate the usefulness** of two sources. It is important to refer to both sources in your answer and also to use your relevant **historical knowledge** to support your answer.

This question is worth 8 marks and you need to allow sufficient time to study the sources thoroughly. Do not forget to also use the **provenance** of the sources!

Types of source (Nature)		
Newspaper article	Speech	Propaganda poster
Diary	Photograph	Political cartoon

Authorship (Origin)		
Government politician	Opposition leader	Foreign journalist
Eye-witness or participant	Local journalist	Common worker

Reasons for existence (Purpose)		
To justify policies	To report events faithfully	To encourage opposition
To challenge establishment	To sensationalise to sell papers	To encourage support

STRETCH IT!

Gather some Nazi propaganda images and political cartoons using online searches. Note two strengths of each and give one enquiry for which they might be useful.

NAIL IT!

Provenance refers to the Nature, Origin and Purpose of a source (NOPe). Always make sure you interrogate a source's caption for this information as well as the source material itself. What does the provenance reveal about how useful a source might be?

Remember, a biased source can still be useful…for the right enquiry!

DO IT!

1 Give a strength and a weakness of each source type given left.

2 Give a strength and a weakness of each example of authorship given left.

3 Give a strength and a weakness of each reason given left.

4 The date a source was published can also affect its usefulness: was it written before, during or after any relevant key events? Name six key dates in this topic and their relevant events.

Re-examine the provenance of the sources from Question 1 for usefulness. (In the exam, you will use different sources from those provided in Question 1.) Key elements are highlighted for you below.

Source B: Nazi propaganda poster promoting annual Winter Relief work in 1938. The caption reads 'Winter Relief Work: A people helps itself'.

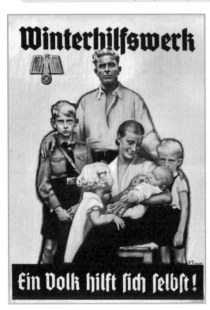

Winterhilfswerk

Ein Volk hilft sich selbst!

Source C: Extract from Hitler's speech to the National Socialist Women's League, 8 September 1934.

> If the man's world is said to be the State, his struggle, his readiness to devote his powers to…the community, then it may perhaps be said that the woman's is a smaller world. For her world is her husband, her family, her children, and her home. But what would become of the greater world if there were no one to tend and care for the smaller one? How could the greater world survive if there were no one to make the cares of the smaller world the content of their lives? No, the greater world is built on the foundation of this smaller world.

Here is the Nature of the source. Here is the Origin.

Here is the Purpose/Audience of the source.

Always note the date a source was produced for any significance.

Enquiries	
What were Hitler's views on family roles?	How did Nazi Germany view the young?
How did women's lives change under the Nazis?	What impact did the Nazis have on living standards?

1 Choose an enquiry from the list above and explain the usefulness of the provenance of each source to that enquiry.

2 Choose another enquiry and explain the usefulness of the *content* of the sources to it.

3 Reorder the enquiries, with the one the sources are most useful for at the top.

4 How useful are these sources to your chosen enquiry overall?

NAILIT!

Remember to compare your own knowledge with the content of the sources. Are there any inaccuracies or omissions that suggest bias or affect usefulness? How knowledgeable was the author and how true a portrayal were they giving?

Look at the exam-style question below.

Edexcel exam-style question

For this question, you will need to use the sources on the previous page.

> **3 (a) Study Sources B and C.**
>
> How useful are Sources B and C for an enquiry into Nazi views about women?
>
> Explain your answer, using Sources B and C and your knowledge of the historical context.
>
> (8)

A strong answer will assess usefulness in the context of the specific enquiry, and will analyse both the provenance and the content of both sources. Contextual knowledge will be used to interpret and assess the sources.

Here are some student notes to answer this question:

> • Source B Provenance: Propaganda - but winter relief, not specifically role of women, 1938
>
> • Source C Provenance: Hitler's speech, to female audience (Women's League), Sept 1934
>
> • Source B Content: Mother and girl's positions versus Man and boys
>
> • Source C Content:

DO IT!

1 Add supporting detail to the first two points in the student plan above to explain how they impact on each source's usefulness to the enquiry.

2 Complete the notes on Source C's content.

3 How does each Source compare to your own knowledge? Write two points for each source.

4 Now try to write a complete answer to the exam-style question above.

NAIL IT!

According to the mark scheme, a strong answer should:

- assess how the provenance (NOPe) of each source affects usefulness
- analyse the content to assess its usefulness
- apply contextual knowledge in interpreting the sources
- come to a reasoned judgement.

Does yours?

Compare your answer to the question on the previous page about how useful Sources B and C are for an enquiry into Nazi views about women with the following student answer.

Source B is a propaganda poster from 1938, well into the Nazi period. As propaganda it is useful for enquiries into Nazi views, as it is state-produced and intended to influence people's opinions. It therefore is likely to reflect accurately what the Nazis wanted people to think. The poster is not directly related to the enquiry of views on women, as it is about a relief programme, but as it shows a German family it is very useful in seeing how Nazis portrayed the 'ideal' German family.

Source B shows a clear contrast between the female and male family members. This is very useful as it clearly shows that men and women were expected to follow separate roles. The mother is sitting down, on a lower level to her husband, surrounded by her four children. Her attention is solely on the baby in her arms, as is the attention of her young daughter. This indicates that women should be focused on their families. Because there are four children, the poster also shows that women should ideally have many children. This matches my own knowledge that women were encouraged not to work through marriage loans and forced out of many professions by the Nazis in order to stay at home and raise families.

Source C is a speech delivered by Hitler in September 1934, one month after becoming Führer of Germany. This is useful because it is Hitler's own views being shared and soon after he had gained total power, so he is probably setting the agenda for his rule to come. It is especially useful as he is speaking to the Nazi Women's League - a presumably loyal, female audience. He is therefore more likely to be speaking freely and openly, honestly.

Source C is doubly useful in what it says about Nazi views about women. It clearly states that women's focus should be on the family and the home: 'the woman's is a smaller world. For her world is...her family, her children'. We know this to be true from the focus in schools on domestic education for girls and from drives to encourage large families, such as the Mother's Cross. It shows how the Nazis viewed women's roles as being extremely important - equal but different to men's: 'the greater world is built on the foundation of this smaller world'.

Note the discussion of both provenance and content.

Note how the student has linked their answer back to the question throughout.

Note where they have added supporting details to show their knowledge and understanding of the context.

 DO IT!

Which of the following levels from the mark scheme would you give this answer?

Level 1 Simple, undeveloped judgement, showing limited comprehension and knowledge.

Level 2 Valid judgement with developed support, comprehension and analysis.

Level 3 Valid judgement with developed reasoning, analysing provenance and content for utility.

Section B: Question 3 (b)

 What is the main difference between these views?

In this question you will need to compare two interpretations and identify the main difference between them. You are looking for a fundamental difference and should use details from each interpretation to support your explanation for this difference.

As the question is only worth 4 marks, you need to be concise and focused in your answer: keep it brief. But do remember to use quotations from the interpretations to back up your answer.

Interpretation 1: From Spartacus Educational site, 'Women in Nazi Germany'.

The decline in unemployment after the Nazis gained power meant that it was not necessary to force women out of manual work. However, action was taken to reduce the number of women working in the professions. Married women doctors and civil servants were dismissed in 1934 and from June 1936 women could no longer act as judges or public prosecutors. Hitler's hostility to women was shown by his decision to make them ineligible to jury service because he believed them to be unable to "think logically or reason objectively, since they are ruled only by emotion".

> This is from a general education site giving an overview of the role of women in Nazi Germany.

> Detail of actions taken against women.

> Evidence of Hitler being hostile towards women.

Interpretation 2: From *Nurturing the Nation to Purifying the Volk*, by M. Mouton, 2009.

When the [Nazis] took power, they tried to erase any ambiguity in women's roles by increasing the number of public ceremonies and [celebrating] mothers for the sacrifices they made for the nation. Almost from their first day in office, the Nazis [swamped] Germans with propaganda exalting motherhood. Government-sponsored advertisements and posters…loudly and publicly proclaimed, "The care of mothers and children is the holiest duty of the entire German *Volk*".

> This is from a book that focuses specifically on Weimar and Nazi family policy: 'Nurturing the Nation' perhaps suggests a focus on motherhood.

> Evidence that women as *mothers* were celebrated.

> Detail of actions taken to celebrate women.

 **DO IT!**

1 Does Interpretation 1 suggest the Nazis were positive or negative towards women?

2 Does Interpretation 2 suggest the Nazis were positive or negative towards women?

3 What do you think is the main difference between the two interpretations?

It is important to focus on the main, key difference between the two interpretations. Look at the exam-style question below relating to the interpretations on the previous page.

Edexcel exam-style question

3(b) Study Interpretations 1 and 2. They give different views on Nazi opinions about women in the years 1933–39.

What is the main difference between the views?

Explain your answer using details from both interpretations.

(4)

Here are some student notes to answer this question:

> • Interpretation 1: negative, focus on employment, general text
> • Interpretation 2: positive, focus on motherhood, book on families

According to the mark scheme, a weaker answer will:

• show limited analysis of surface differences or without direct evidence in support

whereas a stronger answer will:

• analyse the interpretations to give a key difference of view, with support.

Look at this student answer:

> The main difference between Interpretations 1 and 2 is that 1 sees the Nazi view about women as negative and 2 sees the Nazi view about women as positive.

1 Add evidence from the interpretations to support this answer.

2 Rewrite the answer as two short paragraphs, one on each interpretation.

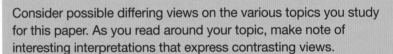

NAIL IT!

Consider possible differing views on the various topics you study for this paper. As you read around your topic, make note of interesting interpretations that express contrasting views.

For example:

• Did Hitler improve living conditions for working Germans?
• Was the popularity of the Nazi Party down solely to Hitler's charisma?
• What was the main reason that Hitler came to power?
• Did the Nazis rule solely through fear?
• Was the Reichstag Fire a deliberate Nazi plot?

Section B: Question 3 (c)

Suggest **one** reason why Interpretations 1 and 2 give different views about…

In this question you will need to suggest a reason for the difference you gave in your answer. You can also use the Sources from Question 3a to help you.

As the question is only worth 4 marks, you need to be concise and focused in your answer: keep it brief. But do remember to use quotations to back up your answer.

Interpretations may differ because historians:

• focus on different sources:

Personal accounts	Economic data	Official records	Newspaper articles

• have a different historical focus:

Economic historian	Social historian	Political historian	Military historian

• have a different perspective:

Long-term view	Local history	Gender history	National history

• have drawn different conclusions from the same evidence:

Given more weight to certain evidence	Focused on role of individuals over masses

DO IT!

1 What different sources might the authors of Interpretations 1 and 2 have emphasised?

2 What different focus might each author have in writing? Do either have 'an agenda'?

3 Are the authors looking with the same perspective?

4 What conclusions have they drawn?

NAIL IT!

Remember you can use the sources from Question 3a to back up your arguments in this question.

Source B shows an 'ideal' German family and Source C discusses men and women's roles.

How can Sources B and C (page 58) support your answer?

Remember you only need to 'suggest **one** reason', but you do need to *explain* that reason. Look at the exam-style question below.

Edexcel exam-style question

3(c) Suggest **one** reason why Interpretations 1 and 2 (page 61) give different views about Nazi views about women.

You may use Sources B and C (page 58) to help explain your answer.

(4)

Here are some student notes to answer this question:

- Interpretation 1: focus on employment: professionals and juries
- Interpretation 1: economic focus, general historical overview
- Interpretation 2: focus on motherhood: public ceremonies and sacrifices
- Interpretation 2: focus on propaganda, family history
- Source B: shows higher status of man over woman
- Source C: Hitler discussing women's separate, but vital, role

According to the mark scheme, a weaker answer will:

- give a simple explanation with limited analysis and support

whereas a stronger answer will:

- give an explanation that analyses the interpretations and provides effective support.

Look at this student answer:

A reason for Interpretations 1 and 2 having different views is because the authors have chosen to each focus on a different aspect of Nazi policy towards women, which encouraged women to focus on their home and family.

1 Add evidence from the interpretations (page 61) to support this answer.

2 Add evidence from the two sources (page 58) to support this answer.

3 Rewrite the answer as two short paragraphs, one on each interpretation.

NAIL IT!

You have 80 minutes in your exam for this paper, which is worth 52 marks in total.

Use the number of marks as a guide for how much time to spend on each question, but remember to allow time for studying the sources and interpretations – and for checking your work at the end.

Section B: Question 3 (d)

 How far do you agree with Interpretation (1 or 2) about...

In this question you will need to evaluate one of the interpretations, and explain 'how far' you agree with it. You must reach a judgement supported by your answer.

This question is worth 16 marks, plus an additional 4 marks for spelling, punctuation, grammar and using specialist historical terms. This is over a third of the total marks, so ensure you leave plenty of time for it.

You will already have assessed the views in the previous questions. Begin with a plan.

STRETCHIT!

Choose one of your course texts and find an extract that provides an opinion on an event you have studied. State the opinion, and give two points in support and two against the view expressed.

State the view in the named interpretation.

Give arguments for it:

- Points from the interpretation

- Points from your own knowledge that support it

Give arguments against it:

- Points from the other interpretation

- Points from your own knowledge that support it

Conclusion:

- It is important to end your answer with a conclusion, based on the evidence for and against.

DOIT!

Complete the following sentence starters to help with your writing. Remember to use linking phrases to lead from one paragraph to the next: this helps give structure to your argument.

1 Interpretation 1 states that...
2 Interpretation 1 supports this view by...
3 From my own knowledge, I would add that...
4 I agree/disagree with this view because...
5 On the other hand, Interpretation 2...
6 Interpretation 2 is supported by...
7 I would challenge/support this because...
8 Overall, I agree/disagree

NAILIT!

Always make sure your writing frequently refers back to the exam question. Incorporate the wording of the question in order to help you with this.

In this question you will also be marked on the quality of your spelling, punctuation and use of grammar. You should also aim to make use of a range of relevant specialist terms for the topic.

There is a range of key terms in this topic, some of them German, so be sure to know them!

Abdication	Anti-Semitism	Armistice	*Autobahn*	Censorship	Communist
Constitution	Depression	*Freikorps*	*Führer*	Hyperinflation	*Kaiser*
Kristallnacht	*Lebensunwertes*	*Mein Kampf*	Persecution	Propaganda	*Putsch*
Rearmament	Reichstag	*Rentenmark*	Reparations	Trade Union	*Untermenschen*

You should also make sure you can spell the key names and remember who they are!

Brüning	Goebbels	Goering	Heydrich
Himmler	Hindenburg	Müller	Niemöller
Röhm	Stresemann	Von Papen	Von Schleicher

DO IT!

1 Add any other key terms and names that you can think of to of to the lists above.

2 Try to think up mnemonics and other tricks to help you remember the spelling: e.g. Stresemann was low stress (one s) but had two Plans (two ns).

3 Read the extract from a student answer on the right. How many errors can you find?

4 What level would you give the student's answer for SPaG using the mark scheme on the right?

Here is an extract from a student answer:

Intrepation X suggests that the Nasis were not responsable for the Richstach Fire. It gives as evidence the fact that Vande Lub was taken away for trial rather than shot imediately. If they needed to silence him he would not have lived to tell I find this argument compeling, as from my own knowlidge - I believe the Nasis reacted to events rather than planned them. However, the scale of propanda and persicusion that followed suggests more planning was involved. Also, the timing suggests it was planned. a month after hitler's appointment as chancelor

The mark scheme gives the following levels for SPaG:

Level 1 Errors in spelling, punctuation and grammar severely hinder meaning.

Level 2 Reasonable accuracy, errors do not significantly hinder meaning, limited use of key terms.

Level 3 Considerable accuracy and control of meaning, with a good range of key terms.

Level 4 Consistent accuracy and effective control of meaning, with a wide range of key terms.

NAIL IT!

Creating revision quizzes and spelling tests, crosswords or other word puzzles for you and your revision buddies is a great way to reinforce your learning.

Make sure you know your acronyms: SS, SD, SA, KPD, SPD etc.

A strong answer will weigh both sides in an argument before coming to a conclusion based on the evidence given: remember, it's not about being right or wrong, it is all about the *argument*! Look at this exam-style question.

Edexcel exam-style question

Spelling, punctuation, grammar and use of specialist terminology will be assessed in part (d).

3(d) How far do you agree with Interpretation 1 (page 61) about Nazi views about women?

Explain your answer, using both interpretations and your knowledge of the historical context.

(16)

(Total for spelling, punctuation, grammar and use of specialist terminology = 4 marks)
(Total for Question 3 = 36 marks)

Here are some student notes to answer the question above:

- View: Hitler hostile
- Interpretation 1: Hitler quote - jury service; jobs in professions
- Own knowledge: (ways women were marginalised)
- Counter view: 'exalted motherhood'
- Interpretation 2: Quote - motherhood; 'erase any ambiguity'
- Own knowledge: (ways women were exalted)
- Judgement:

1 Plan a response to the question above using the structure from the student notes (left).

2 Make a list of key terms and names you might need.

3 Complete the plan by adding some additional knowledge that would support each interpretation.

4 Write a concluding paragraph that gives your judgement.

5 Now write your response in full.

Evidence		
Marriage loans	The Mother's Cross	*Lebensborn* programme
Propaganda posters	Grammar schools for girls	German Women's Enterprise

NAILIT!

According to the mark scheme, a strong answer should:

- provide an explained evaluation of the two opposing views
- give precise analysis of how the views are conveyed
- use evidence and contextual knowledge precisely in support
- reach an overall judgement with coherent, logical reasoning.

Does yours?

Compare your answer to the question on the previous page about how far you agree with Interpretation 1 about Nazi views about women with the following student answer.

Interpretation 1 gives a negative view of Nazi views about women, referring to Hitler's 'hostility to women' and quoting him as saying they "cannot think logically or reason objectively".

The author of Interpretation 1 uses compelling quotes and the argument is somewhat convincing. It focuses on how women were driven out of professional roles such as that of doctors and made ineligible for jury service or to serve as judges and prosecutors. I can further add to this from my own knowledge that the Law for the Enforcement of Marriage offered young couples loans to help support them, but only if the wife stopped working. Also, SS leader Himmler's Lebensborn programme treated young Aryan women simply as breeding stock for loyal Nazi soldiers, while grammar schools for girls were abolished in 1937 - denying them access to university.

To counter this view, it should be pointed out that Hitler's main objective in coming to power was on reducing the six million unemployed. These measures aimed to keep women at home, in the domestic sphere, to free up jobs for German men. Following the Great Depression, there was much suffering and hardship in Germany and the Nazis used this to boost their popularity. They were committed to resolving these issues in order to retain their public support. By 1939, unemployment had fallen to 0.3 million - thanks, in part, to the female 'invisible unemployed' who did not count.

Interpretation 2 gives a much more positive view of Nazi views about women, suggesting the Nazis wished to remove 'any ambiguity' but also 'exalting motherhood' in their propaganda.

The author of Interpretation 2 focuses on women in the role of mothers and convincingly shows how the Nazis celebrated motherhood with ceremonies and praise: 'the holiest duty' of all Germans. I agree strongly that, in this limited sphere, the Nazis had a far more positive view of the role of women. From my own knowledge, I recall that Hitler wanted to encourage large families of loyal Nazis. He did this through awards such as the Mother's Cross for childbirth, making the Hitler Youth salute bearers of the medal. The German Women's Enterprise was formed to promote this role under Reich's Women's Leader Scholtz-Klink, showing women's promotion within their own sphere: as Hitler himself told them, the female sphere was different but no less important to the Third Reich.

However, I would limit this view by referring to the same propaganda that the author mentions. The 'ideal' Nazi family was a common feature of Nazi propaganda. However, the family was usually shown with the men standing tall and proud while the women were seated with the children, a visibly lower status. While the men stare outwards, engaging the reader, the women are focused only on their family. The Nazis had strict views on what Aryan women should look like and act like, and hated the more independent 'new women' of the Weimar days. Even the school curriculum was based solely around domestic skills and preserving racial purity (as well as Party loyalty).

In conclusion, I agree with Interpretation 1 that Nazi views about women were largely negative and that women were denied many opportunities under the Third Reich. However, I also agree with Interpretation 2 that, specifically in the sphere of motherhood, women were 'exalted' and celebrated by the Third Reich.

Note how the student has referred to the interpretations and linked their answer back to the question throughout.

Note where they have flagged supporting information to show their knowledge and understanding of the context.

Finally, a clear conclusion weighs up both sides before making a clear judgement.

DO IT!

1 Which of the following levels from the mark scheme would you give the student answer on page 68?

Level 1 A simple comment with limited analysis of one interpretation, using simple paraphrases or quotes and generalised contextual knowledge.

Level 2 An evaluative comment with analysis and support from both interpretations, using relevant contextual knowledge and providing an undeveloped or unsustained judgement.

Level 3 An explained evaluation with good analysis and support showing the different views. Relevant contextual knowledge is used and an overall judgement is given.

Level 4 An explained evaluation with precise analysis and support showing how the differences of view are made clear. Relevant contextual knowledge is used precisely and an overall judgement is supported by sustained and clear argument.

2 Which of the following levels for SPaG would you award this answer?

Level 1 Errors in spelling, punctuation and grammar severely hinder meaning.

Level 2 Reasonable accuracy, errors do not significantly hinder meaning, limited use of key terms.

Level 3 Considerable accuracy and control of meaning, with a good range of key terms.

Level 4 Consistent accuracy and effective control of meaning, with a wide range of key terms.

SNAP IT!

You can take a photo of the guides to the mark schemes within this section to remind yourself what a good answer for each question type looks like.

STRETCH IT!

Look at the latest sample assessment materials from the Edexcel website and practise answering the sample papers there in exam conditions.

NAIL IT!

Now you have worked through this section on how to answer the exam questions, have a go at the two sample papers that follow. Time yourself to get used to the pressure of exam conditions.

Look back over the descriptions of the mark schemes in this section to assess your answers.

How did you do? Are there any areas in which you need further practice or help? You can focus your revision time on strengthening these areas.

Ask your teacher or look on the Edexcel website for more sample questions to practise.

Practice papers

Answer both questions.

Study Source A below and then answer Question 1.

Source A: A photograph of Nazi 'German Day' in Nuremberg, September 1923. This was a nationalist celebration of military victory over France.

1 Give **two** things you can infer from Source A about Nazi popularity in the 1920s. Complete the table below to explain your answer.

(i) What I can infer:

....

....

   Details in the source that tell me this:

....

....

(ii) What I can infer:

....

....

   Details in the source that tell me this:

....

....

(Total for Question 1 = 4 marks)

2 Explain why there was opposition to the Weimar government in the period 1919–23.

> You may use the following in your answer:
> - The Ruhr crisis
> - The Treaty of Versailles
>
> You **must** also use information of your own.

(Total for Question 2 = 12 marks)

TOTAL FOR SECTION A = 16 MARKS

Practice paper 1: Section B

For this section, you will need to use the sources and interpretations on page 76.

3 (a) Study Sources B and C.

How useful are Sources B and C for an enquiry into the reasons for the popularity of the Nazi Party?

Explain your answer, using Sources B and C and your own knowledge of the historical context.

(8)

(b) Study Interpretations 1 and 2. They give different views about the popularity of the Nazi Party.

What is the main difference between the views?

Explain your answer using details from both interpretations.

(4)

(c) Suggest **one** reason why Interpretations 1 and 2 give different views about the popularity of the Nazi Party.

You may use Sources B and C to help explain your answer.

(4)

Spelling, punctuation, grammar and use of specialist terminology will be assessed in part (d).

(d)   How far do you agree with Interpretation 2 about the popularity of the Nazi Party? Explain your answer, using both interpretations and your knowledge of the historical context.

(16)

(Total for spelling, punctuation, grammar and use of specialist terminology = 4 marks)

(Total for Question 3 = 36 marks)

TOTAL FOR SECTION B = 36 MARKS
TOTAL FOR PAPER = 52 MARKS

Practice paper 2: Section A

Answer both questions.

Study Source A below and then answer Question 1.

Source A: Photograph of the SA standing in front of a Nazi Party office in Berlin, October 1932.

1 Give **two** things you can infer from Source A about the role of the SA in the 1930s. Complete the table below to explain your answer.

> (i) What I can infer:
>
> ....
>
> ....
>
>   Details in the source that tell me this:
>
> ....
>
> ....
>
> (ii) What I can infer:
>
> ....
>
> ....
>
>   Details in the source that tell me this:
>
> ....
>
> ....

(Total for Question 1 = 4 marks)

2 Explain why the late 1920s were seen as the 'Golden Years' of the Weimar Republic.

> You may use the following in your answer:
> - Dawes Plan
> - League of Nations
>
> You **must** also use information of your own.

(Total for Question 2 = 12 marks)

TOTAL FOR SECTION A = 16 MARKS

Practice paper 2: Section B

For this section, you will need to use the sources and interpretations on page 77.

3 (a) Study Sources B and C.

How useful are Sources B and C for an enquiry into the aims of Hitler and the Nazi Party?

Explain your answer, using Sources B and C and your own knowledge of the historical context.

(8)

(b) Study Interpretations 1 and 2. They give different views about the aims of Nazi propaganda.

What is the main difference between the views?

Explain your answer using details from both interpretations.

(4)

(c) Suggest one reason why Interpretations 1 and 2 give different views about the aims of Nazi propaganda.

You may use Sources B and C to help explain your answer.

(4)

Spelling, punctuation, grammar and use of specialist terminology will be assessed in part (d).

(d)   How far do you agree with Interpretation 2 about the aims of Nazi propaganda?

Explain your answer, using both interpretations and your knowledge of the historical context.

(16)

(Total for spelling, punctuation, grammar and use of specialist terminology = 4 marks)

(Total for Question 3 = 36 marks)

TOTAL FOR SECTION B = 36 MARKS
TOTAL FOR PAPER = 52 MARKS

Sources/interpretations for use with Practice paper 1: Section B

Source B: Otto Strasser, *Hitler and I*, 1940. Strasser was an early supporter of Hitler who was expelled from the Party in 1930 for his socialist views and then went into exile.

Adolf Hitler enters a hall. He sniffs the air. For a minute he [fumbles], feels his way, senses the atmosphere. Suddenly he bursts forth. His words go like an arrow to their target, he touches each wound on the raw, [freeing] the mass unconscious, expressing its innermost aspirations, telling it what it most wants to hear…Hitler responds to the vibrations of the human heart with the delicacy of a seismograph*, or perhaps of a wireless receiving set, enabling him…to act as a loud-speaker proclaiming the most secret desires, the least admissible instincts, the sufferings and personal revolts of a whole nation.

*Instrument used to detect and record earthquakes.

Source C: From 1932 Nazi election flyer aimed at supporters of the KPD.

We Nazis help each other. He who has something to eat shares it with him who has nothing. He who has a spare bed gives it to him who has none. That is why we have become so strong. The election shows what we can do. Everyone helps! Everyone sacrifices! The unemployed give up their wedding rings. Everyone gives, even if it is but a penny. Many small gifts become a large one.

Interpretation 1: From *Nazism 1919-45*, by J. Noakes and G. Pridham, 1984.

The image of German society [shown] by Nazi propaganda in newsreels and the press was of mass enthusiasm and commitment. However, in trying to understand what Germans really felt during these years the historian is faced with serious problems. Not only were there no opinion polls but it was impossible for people to express their views in public with any freedom: the result of elections and plebiscites were rigged; the media were strictly controlled. Newspapers are of limited value as a source, since the editors were subject to detailed instructions from the Propaganda Ministry on what to print and were severely [punished] if they stepped out of line. In short, an independent opinion did not exist in the Third Reich.

Interpretation 2: From *Backing Hitler*, by R. Gellately, 2001.

We are used to ignoring the subsequent elections and plebiscites under Hitler's dictatorship, but they tend to show that a pro-Nazi consensus formed and grew. In October 1933 Hitler withdrew Germany from the League of Nations and called a national plebiscite to ask Germans if they agreed. The results were 95 per cent in favour. Hardly less spectacular were the results of the election he called for November…Hitler and his party received almost forty million votes (92.2 per cent of the total). Hardly less remarkable was the turnout of 95.2 per cent of those eligible.

Sources/interpretations for use with Practice paper 2: Section B

Source B: Hitler speaking in 1932.

> The workers have their own parties. The middle class needs even more parties. And the Catholics too, they have their own party. Thirty parties in one little land. And this at a time when before us lie the greatest tasks, which can only be undertaken if the strength of the whole nation is put together. Our enemies accuse us…of intolerance. They are right. We are intolerant. I have given myself one aim: to sweep the thirty parties out of Germany.

Source C: An advert for an anti-Semitic exhibition in Vienna, August 1938. The image shows a caricature (exaggerated portrayal) of a Jew and the caption reads 'The eternal Jew'.

Interpretation 1: From an A-Level textbook by Pearson, 2015.

As early as the 1920s, Hitler was saying that people could be won over to almost anything if it was presented as a simple idea, with a single slogan or image repeated over and over again. For example, 'One People, one Reich, one Führer'…Nazi control of the media enabled them to manipulate what people saw and heard from very early on. For example, they made sure a Nazi reported the reaction to Hitler's appointment as chancellor. He reported huge, cheering torchlight processions in Berlin, with a mass of people chanting 'Sieg Heil!' (the Nazi chant, 'Hail Victory!'). So everyone listening to the radio was immediately convinced of Hitler's huge popularity.

Interpretation 2: From *The Coming of the Third Reich* by R.J. Evans, 2004.

[T]he Nazi propaganda apparatus skilfully targeted specific groups in the German electorate, giving campaigners training in addressing different kinds of audience… providing topics for particular venues and picking the speaker to fit the occasion. [The Party] recognized the growing divisions of German society into competing interest-groups in the course of the Depression and tailored their message to their particular constituency…The Nazis adapted according to the response they received…producing a whole range of posters and leaflets designed to win over different parts of the electorate.

Doing well in your exam

This revision guide is designed to help you with your **Paper 3: Modern depth study** exam.

Section A has an inference question on a source and a causation question.

Section B is accompanied by a **Sources/Interpretations Booklet**.

You will have an answer booklet for Sections A and B and a sources/ interpretations booklet for Section B. Check that you have the correct booklet for the topics you studied.

Assessment objectives

Your answers will be marked according to a mark scheme based on four assessment objectives (AOs). AOs are set by Ofqual and are the same across all GCSE History specifications and all exam boards:

AO1	demonstrate knowledge and understanding of the key features and characteristics of the period studied.
AO2	explain and analyse historical events and periods studied using second-order historical concepts (cause and consequence).
AO3	analyse, evaluate and use sources (contemporary to the period) to make substantiated judgements, in the context of historical events studied.
AO4	analyse, evaluate and make substantiated judgements about interpretations (including how and why interpretations may differ) in the context of historical events studied.

Paper 3, covered in this guide, examines **ALL** the objectives: AO1, AO2, AO3 and AO4. There will also be marks awarded for SPaG (Spelling, Punctuation and Grammar).

You must <u>revise all of the content</u> from the specification as the questions in your exam could be on *any* of the topics listed. This guide is modelled on the specification so make sure you cover **all** the topics in this book.

There are six different types of question to answer in Paper 3:

Question 1	You will be given a contemporary source (a source from the historical period you are studying). You need to infer **two** things from this source by completing a table.
Best answers ...	will support two different inferences with clear details from the source.
(1 marks) 5 minutes	The answer carries 1 marks so you do not have to write much. You will have approximately 5 minutes to answer this question.
Question 2	Asks you to explain why something happened (causation). You will be provided with **two** prompts that you may include.
Best answers ...	will include at least three factors (two could be the prompts). You need to demonstrate both knowledge and understanding and also your ability to analyse causation. Use phrases like 'this led to', 'this meant that', 'consequently' or 'as a result'. You should aim to write a brief introduction and three further paragraphs explaining three factors that help to explain the question.

(12 marks) 15 minutes	You will have approximately 15 minutes to answer this question.
📝 Question 3 (a)	You will be presented with **two** contemporary sources and asked how useful they are to a historian studying a particular event or historical issue.
✒ Best answers …	will refer to the provenance of each source and add some contextual knowledge to reach a conclusion about each source's utility. You could try using the following method to help you remember what to include: **PAST.**

P	Purpose	Ask why the source was produced.
A	Audience	Who did the source address?
S	Situation	Consider the situation of the author.
T	Test	Test against your own knowledge (contextual knowledge).

	You should aim to write two paragraphs for each of the two sources: one on provenance (NOPe) and one on content. You must consider the particular enquiry stated in the question. You are not simply answering 'are the sources useful – in a general sense', the question is more specific than that.
(8 marks) 15 minutes	You will have approximately 15 minutes to answer this question, including time to study the sources.
📝 Question 3 (b)	You will be presented with **two** historical interpretations that give different views about a topic and asked to identify the main difference between these views.
✒ Best answers …	will be focused on a fundamental difference between the two views and will use details from each interpretation in support.
(4 marks) 10 minutes	The answer carries 4 marks so you do not have to write much more than a good-sized paragraph – you will have approximately 10 minutes to answer this question, including time to study the interpretations.
📝 Question 3 (c)	Using the **same two** historical interpretations from Question 3 (b), you will be asked to suggest one reason for the difference between the views.
✒ Best answers …	will be those that analyse the two interpretations and use details from each interpretation in support. You may also draw on the sources from Question 3 (a).
(4 marks) 5 minutes	The answer carries 4 marks so you do not have to write much more than a good-sized paragraph – you will have approximately 5 minutes to answer this question.
📝 Question 3 (d)	Using the **same two** historical interpretations from Questions 3 (b) and (c), you will be asked 'How far do you agree?' with **one** of the interpretations.
✒ Best answers …	will be those that evaluate both interpretations/views, using evidence from the interpretations and also contextual own knowledge, before reaching a coherent overall judgement on the question. You should aim to write two paragraphs on each interpretation: one in support of its view and one against it. It is useful also to write a brief introduction to each interpretation, stating clearly the view that it takes. Finally, it is important to write a final paragraph conclusion to answer the question of 'how far' you agree or disagree with the specified interpretation.
(16 marks + 4 SPaG marks) 30 minutes	This question carries the most marks and therefore you should write the most for this answer. You should aim to spend approximately 30 minutes on this question.

Find past papers and mark schemes, and specimen papers on the Edexcel website at www.qualifications.pearson.com for further practice.

Glossary

abdicate To step down from a position of leadership.

armistice A formal agreement to stop fighting.

autobahn German name for dual-carriage motorways.

castration The removal of male reproductive organs.

causation The reasons why events occurred.

censorship Controlling the content of media such as books, newspapers and films.

communist A left-wing **socialist** revolutionary.

concentration camp A prison camp where large numbers are held in a relatively small space and poor conditions.

consequence The results of events or actions.

constitution The laws or rules that state how a country is governed.

depression A serious and prolonged period of **economic** decline.

factors
> **cultural** Relating to the Arts and ideas of society.
> **economic** Relating to production and income.
> **military** Relating to armed forces and conflict.
> **political** Relating to government and laws.
> **social** Relating to people and society.

fascist Someone who believes in the absolute power of the state over individual freedoms and has little tolerance for opposing views. Fascism is a **political** ideology that developed in Italy and then Germany between the World Wars.

femme fatale An intelligent, beautiful female character that leads men into trouble.

Freikorps 'Free Corps', made up of former soldiers who had kept their weapons.

Führer A German word for leader, Hitler took this title when he combined the roles of Chancellor and President of Germany.

Gestapo Nazi plain clothes secret state police force.

hyperinflation When **inflation** occurs rapidly.

inference Something suggested but not stated directly.

inflation When prices – the cost of living – rises.

interpretation Historical accounts looking back at the past.

Kaiser German 'emperor' or royal leader.

Mein Kampf 'My Struggle', outlined Hitler's **political** ideas and became a bestseller.

nationalist One that supports the interests of their nation often to the detriment of other nations.

Nazi Party Hitler's rebranded right-wing **political** party, the NSDAP.

nazification The spread and encouragement of Nazi ideas and attitudes.

persecution Hostility, usually directed at someone due to their race or beliefs.

propaganda Spreading biased information and ideas to promote a cause.

putsch A violent attempt to overthrow the rightful government.

Reichsrat second of two houses in the Weimar German parliament, the other being the **Reichstag**.

Reichstag German parliament.

Rentenmark New German currency, backed by Germany's gold reserves.

reparations Compensation paid by the losers of a war to the victors.

SA Nazi private army led by Röhm before his murder, the '*Sturmabteilung*', 'Storm Troopers'.

socialist One who believes the role of the state is to benefit the working man.

source Evidence created at the time of the event concerned.

SPD German Social Democratic Party, the largest party in the **Reichstag** in 1918.

SS Hitler's bodyguards, eventually in charge of state security in Nazi Germany, the '*Schutzstaffel*', 'Protection Squad'.

sterilisation Surgery carried out to prevent someone reproducing.

trade union Organised body of workers.